DIRECT HIT

Since 2013, Elon Musk has been at war with car dealers in the United States. Battles have played out in legislative backrooms, courtrooms, governors' offices, and news media outlets across the country. As of now, Musk has won the war. Tesla has established a foothold across the country, sold over two million cars without using a dealer, established a loyal customer base, and overcome most states' franchise dealer laws. *Direct Hit* tells the story of this fight, taking readers into courtrooms and legislative halls where the dealers tried in vain to derail Tesla's advances. The book shares key insights into the strategic choices made by dealers, legacy car companies, and electric-vehicle start-ups. With a combination of historical narrative, blow-by-blow accounts of the Tesla wars, and a consideration of America's longstanding romance with the personal automobile, *Direct Hit* shares a uniquely American drama over cars and the people who sell them.

Daniel A. Crane is the Richard W. Pogue Professor of Law at the University of Michigan. An expert in antitrust law, he has written over 200 books and articles in that field. Since 2014, Professor Crane has been the leading academic voice on the controversies surrounding direct-to-consumer sales of automobiles in the United States.

Direct Hit

HOW TESLA WENT STRAIGHT TO CONSUMERS AND SMASHED THE CAR DEALERS' MONOPOLY

Daniel A. Crane
University of Michigan Law School

Shaftesbury Road, Cambridge CB2 8EA, United Kingdom

One Liberty Plaza, 20th Floor, New York, NY 10006, USA

477 Williamstown Road, Port Melbourne, VIC 3207, Australia

314–321, 3rd Floor, Plot 3, Splendor Forum, Jasola District Centre, New Delhi – 110025, India

103 Penang Road, #05–06/07, Visioncrest Commercial, Singapore 238467

Cambridge University Press is part of Cambridge University Press & Assessment, a department of the University of Cambridge.

We share the University's mission to contribute to society through the pursuit of education, learning and research at the highest international levels of excellence.

www.cambridge.org
Information on this title: www.cambridge.org/9781009687898

DOI: 10.1017/9781009687911

© Daniel A. Crane 2026

This publication is in copyright. Subject to statutory exception and to the provisions of relevant collective licensing agreements, no reproduction of any part may take place without the written permission of Cambridge University Press & Assessment.

When citing this work, please include a reference to the
DOI 10.1017/9781009687911

First published 2026

A catalogue record for this publication is available from the British Library

Library of Congress Cataloging-in-Publication Data
Names: Crane, Daniel A., author.
Title: Direct hit : how Tesla went straight to consumers and smashed the car dealers' monopoly / Daniel A. Crane, University of Michigan Law School.
Description: Cambridge, United Kingdom ; New York, NY : Cambridge University Press, 2026. | Includes bibliographical references and index.
Identifiers: LCCN 2025022334 (print) | LCCN 2025022335 (ebook) | ISBN 9781009687935 (hardback) | ISBN 9781009687911 (ebook)
Subjects: LCSH: Automobile industry and trade – Law and legislation. | Automobile dealers – Legal status, laws, etc. | Direct selling – Law and legislation | Alternative fuel vehicle industry – Law and legislation. | Electric vehicle industry – Law and legislation. | Tesla Motors. | Musk, Elon.
Classification: LCC K3970.A94 C73 2026 (print) | LCC K3970.A94 (ebook) | DDC 381/.45629222–dc23/eng/20250508
LC record available at https://lccn.loc.gov/2025022334
LC ebook record available at https://lccn.loc.gov/2025022335

ISBN 978-1-009-68793-5 Hardback
ISBN 978-1-009-68789-8 Paperback

Cambridge University Press & Assessment has no responsibility for the persistence or accuracy of URLs for external or third-party internet websites referred to in this publication and does not guarantee that any content on such websites is, or will remain, accurate or appropriate.

For EU product safety concerns, contact us at Calle de José Abascal, 56, 1°, 28003 Madrid, Spain, or email eugpsr@cambridge.org

To Elie, Pascal, and Lucian

CONTENTS

Acknowledgments		*page* ix
	Introduction	1
1	The Birth of the Franchised Dealer Model	9
2	Elon Musk's Direct Sales Decision	24
3	The Empire Strikes Back	38
4	It's the Consumer, Stupid!	52
5	Legacies in the Crossfire	72
6	Crony Capitalism in the Motor City	87
7	Strange Bedfellows	105
8	The Others	125
9	How Tesla Turned the Tide	141
10	The Road Ahead	157
Index		171

ACKNOWLEDGMENTS

This book is the culmination of over a decade of academic and public policy work on the direct sales issue. As explained in the Introduction and Chapter 3, I have worked closely on these issues with a wide variety of people, companies, and organizations (although never for compensation).

Among the companies involved, I am particularly indebted for many conversations with people at or affiliated with Tesla, Rivian, Lucid, Aptera, and Scout. Among public interest organizations, I am especially grateful to the Mackinac Center in my home state of Michigan, which has shone a spotlight on the direct sales as an important economic freedom and consumer choice matter. The Electrification Coalition played an important role in bringing together car companies and public interest organizations to advocate on the direct sales issue, and I benefited from many discussions that they organized.

Over the last decade, I have had countless conversations with many other people and companies interested in the direct sales issue. These have included foreign and domestic automobile, truck, and motorcycle manufacturers, environmental organizations, free market groups, consumer protection associations, pro-technology groups, journalists, stock market analysts, elected politicians, academics, Tesla owners organizations, and many others. There are too many to list, but I gratefully acknowledge their many contributions to my thinking and learning for this book.

I wish I could say that I have also had many fruitful conversations with car dealers and their lobbyists. To be sure, I have a few good conversations with the car dealers, but I'm afraid that most of my interactions have been across a table in a legislative session, administrative hearing, or courtroom, or through sparring quotations in Politico, Bloomberg, or the Wall Street Journal. That said, and despite this book, I'm always open for conversation!

Finally, my work as an academic would not be possible without the generous support of the University of Michigan, for which I am very grateful. My research assistant Ginny Miller provided excellent assistance with the preparation of this manuscript.

INTRODUCTION

Anyone who has bought a new car in the last few decades is familiar with the scene: You arrive at a suburban dealership where scores of shiny new models are parked on the lot. Within minutes, you're accosted by an enthusiastic salesperson with well-coifed hair and pearly white teeth who pumps your hand and feigns interest in everything about you from what you do to your children's sports. From there on out, the conversation is oriented around one essential question: "What would it take for you to drive home in your dream car today?" Trade-in? "Let me talk to the shop." Financing? "Give me your driver's license and I can get you an answer in minutes?" Price? "Let me talk to my manager and see what he can do." "Let me think about it" or "I'm still shopping around" aren't acceptable positions. It's the end of the month, or the beginning of the month, or just before a holiday, or right after a holiday, and the dealership is ready to strike a great bargain now or never.

Within the memory of almost every living person, American consumers had to resign themselves that this is just what you had to do if you wanted to buy a car. Buying a new automobile meant haggling with a dealer. If you were a good negotiator – and particularly if you happened to be white and male – you might do OK. Some people actually enjoyed the thrill of manu à manu combat with the pearly white teeth salesman. But most consumers looked forward to dealing with the dealer about as much as to a root canal. The Better Business Bureau receives more complaints about car dealers than about any other business in America, including cable companies and credit agencies.

But why did it have to be this way? After all, consumers were used to buying lots of other products much more flexibly. If you bought a Compaq or Dell computer, it was sold directly to you by Compaq or Dell. If you wanted an iPhone, iWatch, or MacBook, you could buy it over the Internet from Apple, in a company-owned Apple store, in a big-box retailer like Target or Best Buy, or from a phone company like Verizon or AT&T. Even if you bought a huge-ticket item like a new house, you weren't forced to go through a middleman. So what's up with cars?

This book is about how the car dealers got a monopoly over car sales and how one company – Tesla – smashed that monopoly and liberated the American consumer. The story begins in the mid twentieth century, when car dealers were "mom and pop" family-owned businesses that had to deal with an oligopoly of the "Big Three" American car companies – General Motors (GM), Ford, and Chrysler. The dealers complained that they were subject to abusive business practices made possible by the manufacturers' superior bargaining power. It was a period when politicians were especially concerned with protecting small business from exploitation by big business, so these complaints got lots of traction. Every state ended up passing legislation protecting franchised car dealers from their franchising manufacturer. Among the typical protections was a ban on the manufacturer selling or servicing its own cars at retail. Cars would have to be sold to consumers through independent dealers. Direct sales by the manufacturer to the consumer were prohibited.

And that's the way it worked for over half a century. From time to time, a car company would tinker with bypassing the dealers and going straight to consumers, and the car dealers would exercise their political muscle to shut it down. Generations of Americans grew up just assuming that cars had to be bought from dealers, as though that was the proverbial law of the Medes and the Persians, which could never be changed.

But it could, and one man set out to prove it. In 2013, Tesla Motors was going to market with its revolutionary electric vehicle ("EV"), the Model S, which Consumer Reports described as the best car of any kind that it had ever driven. Tesla's founder and CEO, the flamboyant South African-American entrepreneur Elon

Musk, looked at the way that other car companies sold cars through burdensome dealer networks and announced that the 1950s distribution model wasn't going to work for Tesla. If the company was going to succeed in achieving mass-market penetration of its EVs, it would have to sell those cars directly to consumers and provide warranty and other servicing itself. Customers might buy Teslas over the Internet, or they might visit company-owned retail and service centers, but franchised dealers with their high-pressure sales tactics would be nowhere in the picture.

Of course, the dealers weren't one bit happy about this. Since before World War II, they had enjoyed legal protection from this kind of competition from manufacturers. They had made investments in dealerships on the assumption that they would perpetually enjoy the benefits of state dealer protection laws. For a car company to claim the right to bypass the dealers and sell directly to consumers posed an existential threat to the dealers' way of life. And so they struck back against Tesla with a vengeance. State by state across the country, the car dealers employed every legal device at their disposal – litigation, administrative hearings, lobbying legislatures to pass new laws – to keep Tesla from gaining a beachhead and disrupting the status quo.

Though the dealers would go on to win individual battles, and although direct sales remain prohibited in some states as of the writing of this book, this was never a war the dealers could win in the long run. Too much had changed in American society since the 1950s when the dealer protection laws took root. The Big Three had lost their grip over the American car market and were no longer the juggernauts of the mid twentieth century. Most of the dealers were no longer family-owned "mom and pops," but sprawling, multi-million- or multi-billion-dollar businesses. In fact, many dealer groups had more annual revenue than some car countries. The case for laws protecting the dealers from the car companies had long expired. Moreover, long gone were the days when American voters were interested in protecting businesses at the expense of consumers. And, most fundamentally, the economics of EV sales dictated a new distribution model. Franchised dealer sales worked OK for the internal-combustion generation, but forcing that model onto the new generation of all-electric cars would dramatically slow consumer adoption of EVs, to the detriment of the environment and American energy independence. On the merits, the deck was overwhelmingly stacked against the dealers.

One important question is not why the dealers lost, but why were they able to hold out for so long against innovation? As this book will show, that story reveals how economic special interests can use political processes to benefit themselves at the expense of consumers and how, once entrenched, it's difficult to dislodge them. It's no coincidence that the successful challenge to the dealers' monopoly was mounted by the world's wealthiest man – someone who could make the huge investment of resources necessary to fight a multi-state battle against one of the most powerful lobbies in America. The role of Tesla and Elon Musk in the dealer wars makes this story quite different from run-of-the-mill cases where economic special interests capture political processes. It's not a David vs. Goliath story, but Goliath vs. Goliath. Further, as Musk has come to be identified with right-wing politics in recent years, the politics of direct sales have become unusually complicated.

But the cast of characters in this story is not limited to the direct combatants. Tectonic shifts of the kind occasioned by the transition from internal combustion to electric motors affected all sorts of other interests too. Many other players joined the fray. Ford and especially GM decided to come in on the side of the dealers, a decision that was driven by fear of offending their dealer networks and by an effort to prevent Tesla from gaining a foothold in the market with a more efficient distribution method. But it was a call that was at least wrong and may yet prove disastrous. By aligning themselves with the dealers' losing cause, the legacies lost their chance to argue that they too should be allowed to sell EVs directly to consumers. As Tesla continued to roll up wins across the country, the legacies found themselves in the worst possible position. Tesla could sell EVs directly, and the legacies could not. One could point out the injustice of this position, but it was ultimately one of the legacies' own making.

Another important group of participants in the Tesla wars is public interest groups. Unlike many political issues where public interest organizations on the right and the left face off, there has been near unanimity of support for Tesla and direct sales among both liberal and conservative public interest organizations. Environmental groups such as the Sierra Club and Environment America have supported Tesla because they understand that allowing EV manufacturers to sell and service their own cars is critical to mass-market adoption of EVs and flipping the fleet from internal combustion to electric. Consumer groups such as the Consumer Federation of America and Consumer Action have supported Tesla because they aren't huge fans of car dealers and think consumers should have choices about how they buy their cars. And conservative groups like the Koch brothers' Americans for Prosperity and the Institute for Justice have argued in favor of permitting direct sales on free market grounds. Uncharacteristically, some of these usually antagonistic groups have even been willing to work together on this issue, as when the Sierra Club and Americans for Prosperity made national headlines (and ruffled some of their constituents' feathers) by joining the same letter in support of Tesla. At a time when Americans are deeply and bitterly divided on political and social issues, the story of the Tesla wars shows that it's still possible to find common ground.

A last set of important players in our story are the new generation of EV start-ups that are just coming to market. Since the earliest days of the internal combustion revolution, there has never been such a proliferation of new entrants to the car market as there has been in the last few years. Start-up companies such as Rivian, Lucid, Aptera, and Scout are bringing out innovative new lines of electric or solar-powered cars. Others are aiming to create electric medium and heavy-duty trucks for commercial fleets. Almost all of them agree with Tesla that selling directly to buyers is essential to the success of their companies. In many ways, Tesla has paved the way for their success by opening the door to direct sales in many states. But coming second also has its disadvantages. Some of Tesla's victories have been legislative carve-outs for Tesla alone. That means that, in some states, the second generation of EV start-ups will have to fight the Tesla wars all over again. At least they will know the template.

As of this book's writing, the battles between the car dealers and the EV start-ups continue to be waged in many states across the country, and it's too early to say exactly how and when it will all end. However, this much is clear: Tesla won. Tesla's website shows that it has sales centers in thirty-six states (and the District of Columbia) and service centers in thirty-four states. Given that this list includes the twenty largest states by population, the overwhelming majority of American consumers now have access to a Tesla sales or service center in their state. Tesla has sold over two million cars in the United States, not one of them through a dealer. American consumers are becoming used to having the choice of buying cars directly from manufacturers and are liking it. Tesla has consistently beat out traditional car companies in customer satisfaction surveys. Freed from the car dealers' monopoly, consumers are not going to accept being forced back into it.

However the story of the Tesla revolution ends, it is inconceivable that automobile distribution will go back to the 1950s model. Tesla's forceful advancement of the direct sales model is closing a long chapter in the storied history of the American automobile. Franchised car dealers may remain a feature of American life for a long time to come, but consumers will have choices to buy cars in other, more flexible ways.

This book tells the story of how the franchised dealer system came to be, and how Tesla beat it. It begins in Chapter 1 with the early years of mass-produced internal combustion engine automobiles and the business and political decisions that led to a one-size-fits-all model of independent dealer distribution. The story then shifts in Chapter 2 to the advent of Tesla in the early 2010s, and Elon Musk's decision that Teslas would have to be sold and serviced directly by Tesla itself. Chapter 3 recounts the mobilization of the car dealers' lobby to oppose the direct sales model and explores the political reasons that the dealers were able to mount such formidable resistance. Chapter 4 dispels the dealers' self-serving argument that prohibiting direct sales is actually in the interest of consumers. The disastrous response of the legacy car companies – particularly GM – is covered in Chapter 5. The Tesla wars have played out on a state-by-state basis across the country, and Chapter 6 takes a deep dive into one of the more interesting case studies – the car dealers' futile battle to keep Tesla out of Michigan. In Chapter 7, we meet the "strange bedfellows" coalition of environmentalist, consumer, and free market groups that came together to support direct sales. Chapter 8 turns to the next wave of EV start-ups that drafted in Tesla's wake. Chapter 9 recounts how Tesla turned the tide through a combination of legislative, judicial, administrative, and business tactics. Finally, the last chapter looks ahead to the battles still to be fought and offers some thoughts about the future shape of the American automobile industry and the role of dealers.

A final word of introduction goes to my own role in this story. Throughout this book, I will offer stories and perspectives that I gleaned from being in the ring in the Tesla wars. Here's how it happened: I am a law professor who specializes in antitrust law, which concerns competition and market regulation. My academic position happens to be at the University of Michigan, right next door to what was once the car capital of the world. In 2014, I read a news story about one of Tesla's early battles with the car dealers' lobby in New Jersey. At the time, I knew very little about state laws regulating automobile distribution. I was intrigued by the arguments about whether Tesla should be allowed to sell directly to consumers. While I had no dog in the fight about whether selling through independent franchised dealers or directly to consumers was a better strategy for manufacturers or consumers, the arguments that the dealers were making about why the law should *prohibit* direct sales were contrary to fundamental economic principles. After I dug in a bit, what was going on became quite clear: The dealers were trying to leverage antiquated laws grounded in economic circumstances that had long since passed to block innovation in distribution methods for the sale of a new technology – EVs.

At that fateful moment, I publicly weighed in supporting Tesla, and soon found myself in the middle of a political maelstrom taking place in legislatures, courthouses, regulatory agencies, and the court of public opinion across the nation. In the following decade, I worked closely with not only Tesla but also other EV start-ups such as Rivian and Lucid and a variety of environmental, consumer, and free market public interest organizations to make the case for consumers' right to buy directly from the manufacturer. I testified before legislatures and motor vehicle commissions, wrote court briefs, open letters, white papers, and academic articles, appeared on television and radio shows and podcasts, and spoke with countless journalists, legislators, public officials, and members of the public. Before long, I became the unofficial guru of the direct sales movement.

In all that time, I never accepted a penny of compensation for my work. I've worked closely *with* Tesla, Rivian, Lucid, and many other companies, but never *for* them. My goal is not to promote Tesla, other car companies, or even EV technology. It's to help free the American consumer from outdated laws that restrict their choices about how to buy cars.

Whether or not you share my vision for direct sales, I hope you'll find the story of the Tesla wars illuminating.

1 THE BIRTH OF THE FRANCHISED DEALER MODEL

Sigmund and Rose Strochlitz were born in Poland at the beginning of the twentieth century.[1] It was a bad time and place to be Jewish. The Strochlitzes lost most of their families during the Holocaust and narrowly escaped with their own lives. Sigmund survived Auschwitz and then met Rose in the Bergen Belsen concentration camp – just one of many stories about love springing from the ashes of hate. After being liberated by the British army at the end of the war, Sigmund and Rose spent a few years as stateless refugees in Europe. A family legend has it that, while they were courting, Sigmund took Rose for a ride on a moped, didn't know how to stop it, and had to drive it around for a few hours until the machine ran out of gas.

In 1951, the Strochlitzes arrived in New York speaking little English and knowing nothing about cars (or mopeds, apparently). Despite their lack of an automotive background, within a few years of arriving in New York, they had put together enough money to invest in a Ford dealership on Long Island. They never did learn much about cars, but they built the business on personal relationships and honesty. By 1967, the business was doing so well that Ford offered them a prestigious franchise in Manhattan. Turning down both the wealth and burden of a Manhattan lifestyle, the Strochlitzes instead sold their Long Island dealership and bought Whaling City Ford in New London, Connecticut.

It wasn't easy for the big-city immigrants to establish their business in a small New England town. Shortly after their arrival, Sigmund had to deal with an unfortunate incident in which one of Whaling City's mechanics defrauded a customer by falsifying the repairs on a car and pocketing the money. When Sigmund found out about it, he did everything he could to appease the irate customer, including offering to fix the vehicle properly for free and to pay compensation. The customer refused mollification and held out to get Whaling City Ford into serious trouble. While Sigmund was sweating over what might happen next, he happened to get a visit from a prominent New London attorney, who asked Sigmund to lunch to welcome him to the town's business community. Over lunch, the attorney asked whether Sigmund might be interested in heading up one of the town's charities, and Sigmund graciously accepted. A few weeks later, Sigmund again ran into the lawyer. This time, the lawyer explained his real motivation for asking Sigmund to lunch. He had been approached by the irate customer about suing Whaling City. Before deciding on whether to take the case, he had wanted to see what kind of a man Sigmund was. Now that he knew, he had told the customer that neither he nor any other lawyer in town would take a lawsuit against Whaling City. Sigmund had passed his first big test.

For the next twenty years, Sigmund and Rose ran the dealership through good times and bad. During the oil crisis, the Strochlitzes managed to avoid laying off any of their fifty employees by giving everyone – including themselves – a pay cut. Sigmund's office at the dealership was more than the heart of the dealership. It was the heart of the New London community where the United Way, United Jewish Federation, and much of New London's business was done.

In 1986, Sigmund told the family that he wanted to retire. His daughter and son-in-law, who had careers as a doctor and a lawyer, respectively, gave up their professional careers in order to take over the family business, which they ran for another thirty years. When Sigmund passed away, the mayor of New London made a special exception to allow his hearse to pass through downtown. The Strochlitzes had gone from Holocaust survivors and refugees to pillars of the community. And they had done it by being car dealers who knew little about cars. Selling cars was about taking care of people, and on that score, the Strochlitzes were second to none.

The Strochlitzes' story is uniquely their own, but it is also characteristic of the American car dealer in the twentieth century. For much of that century, the car dealership was nearly synonymous with a family-owned small-town business. Dealerships were not only local retailers, they were the beating heart of thousands of towns across America. In the twentieth century, the American story was bound up with the romance of the automobile and the open road, and "mom and pop" car dealers were at the center of that narrative.

Though this story may seem familiar, it was far from inevitable. The franchised dealer model of car distribution was only one of many different ways that cars could be and were sold and serviced. Although the first independent franchise contract for automobile distribution was established by General Motors (GM) for the sale of steam automobiles in 1898,[2] for the first few decades of the twentieth century, manufacturers employed a wide variety of other distribution methods. These included direct distribution through factory-owned stores and traveling salesmen, and distribution through wholesalers, retail department stores, and consignment arrangements.[3] For example, between 1908 and 1912, Sears, Roebuck and Company sold 3,500 Chicago-manufactured automobiles through the Sears Company catalogue.[4] The 25-mile-per-hour, 14-hp two-cylinder engine car arrived in a wooden crate, with the customer responsible for assembly, installation of wheels, and the addition of oil. Montgomery Ward also had a mail-order business for cars. On the lower end of the retail market, C.C. Housenick, a Bloomsburg, Pennsylvania clothing store, sold Stutz, Hudson, Overland, International, and Ford cars from over its shirt counter.[5]

Despite the variety in distribution methods during this period, the predominant way that manufacturers got their cars into the hands of consumers was through short-term contract with a wholesaler, who typically covered an exclusive territory.[6] The wholesalers then subcontracted to retailers, who sold the car to the ultimate consumer. Cars were simple, and so were the distribution agreements. Dealers sold cars and did little else. They provided almost nothing in the way of showrooms, service, repair, or replacement parts.[7]

In the early years, distribution wasn't a principal concern for car manufacturers. Demand vastly outstripped supply, so their principal challenge was producing enough vehicles to meet the growing and voracious demand for this new form of transportation. However, as Ford-pioneered assembly-line production allowed supply to begin matching demand, the car became a mass-produced commodity, and as automobile consumption intensified, the manufacturers found it increasingly necessary to give serious thought not only to how their cars would be built but also to how they would be sold. Beginning in the 1920s, the manufacturers began to move toward a franchised dealer model in order to focus on their core competency in manufacturing and find additional sources of capital to fund their distribution operations.[8]

In his memoir published in 1963, Alfred P. Sloan, GM's iconic CEO and father of modern corporate management, described the factors that led him to push GM toward franchised dealers as the company's principal distribution strategy. Sloan explained that "the experience of the 1920s, when the modern problems of automobile distribution took shape, taught me that a stable dealer organization is a necessary condition for the progress and stability of an enterprise in this industry."[9] While many car manufacturer managers "minimized the role of the dealer," Sloan saw strong relationships between the manufacturers and the dealers as vital to GM's success. Especially when used cars came into the picture and trade-ins became a feature of the new car sales transaction, it was no longer feasible for manufacturers to meet their customers directly.

Sloan outlined two essential characteristics or functions of dealers. First, "the dealer makes the direct personal contact with the customer; he makes and closes the deal that sells the car."[10] The individual franchised dealer was "usually a substantial businessman in his local community" and could meet the customer "often as a neighbor."[11] In a commercial world increasingly characterized by large, impersonal, and distant manufacturers, dealers solved a problem of trust. Second, the franchised dealer occupied a position between that of an independent merchant and an agent of the manufacturer. The dealer was expected to make a large investment in promoting the manufacturer's brand and servicing and supporting its vehicles. Manufacturers and dealers needed to be partners in selling and servicing cars, and that implied a special relationship between them: "Both the dealer and the manufacturer in their relationship have special rights and undertake special obligations."[12]

During the 1920s and early 1930s, Sloan made it a practice to visit regularly with his dealers. He outfitted a private railroad car as an office and, together with a group of other "GM" executives, traveled the country meeting five to ten dealers a day at their own places of business. At these meetings, he would ask for the dealers' criticisms and suggestions about their relationship with the company, GM cars, the company's policies, trends in consumer demand, and their view of the future.[13] Looking back on this experience years later, Sloan reflected that "[t]his time- and effort-consuming approach to the problem was particularly effective under the circumstances existing at that time, when we knew so little about the facts of distribution in the field."[14]

Whatever dealer goodwill Sloan may have achieved through his itinerant outreach didn't last long. By the late 1930s, the relationship between the manufacturers and dealers had begun to sour. Sloan's counterpart Henry Ford may have poisoned the well as early as 1921 when, despite a deep recession, Ford kept its factories running at full tilt and required its dealers to purchase cars that their customers hadn't ordered and the dealers had little chance of selling.[15] In 1929, when the Great Depression hit and automobile purchases fell by 75 percent, Ford again resorted to the same strategy, threatening its dealers with termination (and a loss of their significant capital investments) if they did not purchase unwanted and unsellable cars.[16] Then, when Model T sales began lagging, Ford undercut its existing dealers by setting up new dealers in their backyards in effort to stimulate sales through competition.[17]

These early abuses by Ford, and similar (although mostly later) stories as to GM, would live long in the dealers' memories, but forces larger than particular managerial decisions by the car companies were at work to strain the manufacturer–dealer relationships that Sloan had worked so assiduously to cultivate. As a result of technological, managerial, and economic change, the car industry was consolidating, but very unevenly. At the dealer level, the Depression had a devastating effect, wiping out nearly half of the dealers. Just on the eve of the Depression, the number of dealers peaked in 1927 at 53,125, then dropped by almost half during the Depression to 30,110 in 1945.[18] (The numbers rebounding to a relatively stable range in the 40,000s during the postwar boom years and then trailing down to the 20,000s by the 1980s).[19] The dealers that survived were wary and anxious about their economic position and relationship with the manufacturers.

But it was at the manufacturer level that consolidation was most dramatic. Between 1900 and 1920, over 600 separate companies attempted to produce an automobile.[20] Most were small, undercapitalized companies that produced only a few cars and eventually failed.[21] By the 1930s, the automobile industry had consolidated into the familiar idea of a "Detroit Big Three," with GM, Ford, and Chrysler's multi-vehicle, multi-brand conglomerates dominating the market after mergers (such as Ford/Lincoln in 1922, Chrysler/Dodge in 1928, and GM/Opel in 1929–31) and competitor failures. Between the 1920s and Tesla's entry with the Model S in 2012, not a single mass-market American car manufacturer successfully entered the market – a point memorably underscored by Francis Ford Coppola's 1988 comedy drama *Tucker: The Man and His Dream*. Of course, that period saw plenty of entry into the US market from Asia and Europe, but a near-century without any homegrown start-ups is a curiosity searching for an explanation. The dominance of the Big Three and their respective labor unions are important parts of that story, but so are the franchise dealership laws on which this book is focused.

In sum, over the 1920s–30s, the automobile market shifted from one characterized by a large number of manufacturers struggling for a market position and a far larger number of dealers struggling to gain their own footing, to one in which a much-reduced number of surviving dealers faced up to the new reality of a triopoly of powerful manufacturers. It was that economic shift that gave rise to the legal and political battles between the dealers and manufacturers that played out between the 1930s and 1950s, which in turn set the stage for the franchise dealer laws that were on the books at the time of Tesla's arrival.

In stark juxtaposition to Detroit's manufacturing titans, the 30,000–40,000 dealerships in existence during the Depression, War, and post-war eras were mostly small, family- or locally owned "mom and pops" businesses.[22] If you want a mental image of the traditional local car dealership, picture Whaling City Ford in New London, Connecticut, and Sigmund and Rose Strochlitz, who we met at the beginning of this chapter. Car dealerships were owned by families, often in small towns. The franchise often bore the family name, and it was typically passed on from father to son.

The Birth of the Franchised Dealer Model 15

In the mid twentieth century, the car dealership rightly developed a reputation as a source of economic opportunity, local enterprise, and small-town values. The car dealer could be pitted in a David vs. Goliath narrative against the gigantic, cold-hearted manufacturers in the big city of Detroit and their New York bankers. This narrative played out during a Neal Deal period concerned with reining in the power of large companies and protecting small, independent businesses. This was the era in which (later) Supreme Court Justice Louis Brandeis declared bigness a "curse,"[23] the National Industrial Recovery Act of 1933 replaced antitrust laws with "codes of fair competition," and Congress passed the Robinson-Patman Act of 1936 to halt the power of chain stores like the Great Atlantic & Pacific Tea Company ("A&P").

Early in the twentieth century, the dealers had developed a collective business consciousness which, as economic pressures grew during the Depression, grew into a political consciousness. In 1917, the dealers formed the National Association of Automobile Dealers ("NADA") for explicitly political purposes: Thirty dealers from state and local car dealers associations traveled to Washington, set up camp at the Willard Hotel, and lobbied Congress for relief from total factory conversion to wartime work and a luxury tax on automobiles.[24] In 1941, the organization moved from Detroit to Washington to keep closer tabs on Congress. Over time, NADA began to play an increasing role in the skirmishes, battles, and outright wars between the dealers and Big Three that played out in the 1930s–50s.

The earliest legal skirmishing between the dealers and manufacturers involved lawsuits in which the dealers argued that their franchise agreements were contracts of adhesion – one-sided contracts offered on a take-it-or-leave-it basis – whose harsh terms shouldn't be enforced.[25] The dealers made little headway with these arguments in the courts. And so they turned their attention to two federal bodies that offered the potential for sweeping relief against the Big Three – the United States Congress and the newly minted Federal Trade Commission ("FTC"). In response to dealer pressure, the FTC opened a sweeping investigation of the car distribution market, culminating in a 1077-page report released in 1939.[26] The report brought both good and bad news for the dealers.

On the good side, the FTC documented in painstaking detail a history of abuses of the dealers by the Big Three. A section of the report covered "inequitable requirements imposed on dealers," such as cancellation clauses that prevented the dealers from recovering their investments and orders binding on the dealer but not the manufacturer.[27] Of special concern to the Commission were the dealers' allegations that "Chrysler, General Motors, and Ford have often been particularly ruthless in forcing their dealers to take more cars and trucks than can be sold at a profit."[28] The report quoted at length dealer complaints about being strong-armed into taking unwanted inventory, such as the following July 1938 quote from a Chrysler-Plymouth dealer:

> [W]e were told that we had to buy four Chrysler Imperials, that we had to take our full allotment of this type. This type was unusually hard to sell but the factory threatened that they "would not play ball with us when the new cars come out." There was no other alternative but to take these cars, which we sold at a loss.[29]

A Ford dealer offered a similarly grim accusation: "Coercion has been the practice in the past rather than the exception ... I formerly worked for the Ford Motor Co. ... and have been a roadman. It have been both a 'coercer' and 'coercee.' Cars, tools, and parts have all been forced upon me by threats."[30] The Commission concluded by finding that its "inquiry has demonstrated that inequities exist in the terms of dealer agreements, and in certain manufacturers' treatment of some dealers, calling for remedial action."[31] It suggested legislation providing dealers "less restriction upon the management of their own enterprises"; "quota requirements and shipments of cars based on mutual agreement"; "equitable liquidation in the event of contract termination by the manufacturer"; and "contracts definite as to the mutual rights and obligations of the manufacturers and the dealers."[32]

Unfortunately for the dealers, the FTC also turned the tables and accused *the dealers* of various anticompetitive or anti-consumer practices, such as "padding" new car prices, price fixing, and "packing" finance charges.[33] This was hardly the news the dealers wanted, since it seemed to create a moral equivalence between the manufacturers and the dealers and threatened to stymie their crusade for Congressional legislation to reign in the manufacturers. Acting on the FTC report, the Justice Department did bring antitrust charges against the Big Three, with Chrysler and Ford quickly signing consent decrees and GM losing at trial,[34] but the dealers' crusade in Washington had clearly hit a speed bump. Despite persistent lobbying of Congress, the dealers reaped no federal rewards during the New Deal. They did finally secure a modest federal victory with the Automobile Dealers' Day in Court Act of 1956, which allows dealers to bring a federal suit against a manufacturer who, without good faith, fails to comply with the terms of a franchise agreement or terminates, cancels, or refuses to renew a franchise.[35] However, the broad legislative response to the manufacturers' abuses of their unequal bargaining power sought by the dealers never materialized.

The dealers fared considerably better in the states. In 1937, Wisconsin became the first state to enact an automobile franchise dealer law. Responding to the major concern that would soon be addressed in the FTC's report, the statute prohibited manufacturers from "induc[ing] or coerc[ing] or attempting to induce or coerce any automobile dealer to accept delivery of any motor vehicle or vehicles, parts or accessories therefor, or any other commodities which shall not have been ordered by said dealer."[36] The statute also prohibited manufacturers from doing other unfair acts to dealers by threatening to cancel their contract or cancelling a distribution agreement without due regard to the equities. As the Wisconsin Supreme Court has explained, the Wisconsin legislature enacted the statute in "recognition of the gross disparity of bargaining power between the manufacturer of automobiles and the local retailer," and "the long history of the abuse of dealers by manufacturers."[37] The "purpose of the law is to furnish the dealer with some protection against unfair treatment by the manufacturer."[38]

Following Wisconsin's lead, from the late 1930s forward, states began to pass statutes governing automotive franchise relations.[39] Many states followed the Oklahoma model from 1953.[40] Oklahoma adopted the thrust of Wisconsin's statutes on coercive dealing and wrongful termination, but also added a seven-member Motor Vehicle Commission, staffed by car dealers, to administer the act. Stewart Macaulay, a Wisconsin law professor who studied manufacturer and dealer relations in the 1960s wrote that "[i]n effect, a group of established automobile dealers sits in judgment on other dealers and on manufacturers and their representatives rather than an independent state agency as in Wisconsin. Clearly, this Commission will have a certain type of 'expertise.'"[41] (With the benefit of hindsight, we might add that a commission staffed by automobile dealers might also have a certain type of bias in favor of automobile dealers.)

Between 1937 and 1957, eighteen states passed laws protecting car dealers from manufacturers.[42] Over the next few decades, the other states joined in too. Today, such dealer protection laws are on the books in all fifty states.[43] Their terms vary, but they commonly include prohibitions on forcing dealers to accept unwanted cars, protections against termination of franchise agreements, restrictions on granting additional franchises in a franchised dealer's geographic market area, and manufacturer warranty reimbursement requirements.[44]

The dealer protection provisions that laid the foundation for the Tesla wars, and hence the ones of most interest to this book, prohibit or limit a manufacturer from distributing its cars directly to consumers, effectively requiring the manufacturer to deal exclusively through dealers.[45] Although direct sales by manufacturers were not a major focus of the FTC report, the issue was among the dealer complaints:

> A dealer from the Middle West stated, in effect, that he was one of the two dealers in his city representing a certain division of General Motors Corporation and that he purchased the business of his competitor. He had an oral agreement with the regional manager to the effect that another dealer handling the same line would not be placed in the city. However, within 2 years, the General Motors Holding Co. opened a retail sales outlet for the same line of cars and the company-owned dealer made overallowances when taking used cars in trade on new-car deals. The complaining dealer also stated he experienced difficulty in obtaining delivery of salable models, while at the same time, the company-owned dealer was receiving similar models, and that deliveries to the complaining dealer would be delayed for months while the company dealer would receive immediate deliveries.[46]

By the time that the states began to pass dealer protection laws in the 1930s, company-owned retail stores were already a rarity. For example, in 1916, Ford's management considered a proposal to open twenty-three new company-owned retail branches in larger cities (defined as those with 100,000 or more residents), as both "a profitable venture" and as "indemnification against some of the practice of the larger [independent] agents which mitigate against the service which the Ford Company is anxious to give owners of Ford cars."[47] However, management made the decision that "the Ford Motor Company could not continue to do both retail and wholesale business in the future owing to the company's great growth."[48] Even without the coercion of law, the Big Three had largely made the decision that they would be better off distributing through independent franchised dealers rather than trying to sell cars to consumers directly.

Nonetheless, car companies occasionally did experiment with opening company-owned stores, and the dealers didn't like it. The legislative history of the statutes banning direct sales reflects a concern that if a manufacturer integrated forward into distribution, it might compete unfairly with its own franchised dealers by undercutting them on price.[49] For example, the legislative history of the Michigan statute reveals that the statute was designed to address "the unequal power balance between dealers and manufacturers [that] leaves a great potential for arbitrary and unilateral decisions by manufacturers about contract arrangements"[50] in part by forbidding manufacturers "to compete with franchised dealers by offering the same services."[51] Similarly, the legislative history of Texas' direct sales ban "indicates the legislature's intent to prevent manufacturers from utilizing their superior market position to compete against dealers in the retail car market. The legislature's concern was fueled by the recent opening of several dealerships owned by manufacturers and the perceived detriment to the public from vertical integration of the automobile market."[52]

The direct sales prohibitions came in a number of different forms. Some states, like Connecticut, Louisiana, and Texas, flatly prohibited a manufacturer to own a dealership or otherwise operate a retail store in the state. Other states, like Virginia, Kentucky, and Wisconsin, prohibited a manufacturer from owning a dealership without a determination by the Motor Vehicle Commission that "there is no dealer independent of the manufacturer or distributor, factory branch or distributor branch, or subsidiary thereof available in the community to own and operate the franchise in a manner consistent with the public interest."⁵³ California followed the most permissive model, allowing a manufacturer to open its own retail store so long as it did not place it within ten miles of one of its existing franchised dealers. As Tesla would discover, the direct sales bans came in many varieties, and the state-by-state variance would create both challenges and opportunities for a car company seeking to sell its own cars to consumers.

Although the direct distribution prohibitions came about in different forms and were not all were part of the original state dealer protection laws, they all had a common provenance in the state dealer protection movement that began in Wisconsin in 1937. Significantly for contemporary debates over direct sales, these prohibitions were expressly justified as part of a package of protections for dealers against the exercise of superior manufacturer bargaining power. Manufacturers were assumed to pursue franchisee relationships – since the Big Three all did – and pure direct distribution, where a manufacturer chose not to employ independent dealers at all but go directly to the public – was not considered or discussed. Further, contrary to much later efforts by the dealers to frame these direct distribution prohibitions as consumer protection measures, there is not a whiff of consumer protection sentiment in these statutes. They were all about protecting *dealers* in franchise relationships from the exigencies of superior manufacturer bargaining power.

How did the Big Three take these laws? For most of the twentieth century, the direct sales prohibitions were the least of their concerns. They had largely decided to pursue a dealer distribution strategy anyway, and other aspects of the state dealer protection laws (e.g., those limiting their power to terminate underperforming dealerships) were of much greater concern. Occasionally, one of the Big Three would think about experimenting with some form of direct sales, only to be beaten back by the car dealers and their allies in the motor vehicle commissions. For example, in the late 1990s, Ford decided to try its hand at the growing e-commerce market for used cars and launched www.fordpreowned.com which allowed customers in Houston, Atlanta, Boston, Washington D.C., New York, and Newark to buy used Fords that had previously been leased by Ford dealer to a consumer, sold or leased by Ford to national car rental companies, or used as company service vehicles by Ford employees. Customers could make a $300 refundable deposit and then test drive the car at a local dealership. The customer could then elect to purchase the car for a "no-haggle" price determined by Ford and listed on the website. Upon payment or financing approval, Ford would transfer title to the dealer, who, in turn would transfer title to the customer and then get paid a commission by Ford. The Texas Motor Vehicle Board found that even this limited form of direct sales, in which a dealer played a role for compensation, violated Texas' direct sales prohibition. Ford brought a constitutional challenge in federal court and lost in the court of appeals.[54]

For the most part, the Big Three and their foreign competitors acquiesced in the vertical disintegration system established by the dealer franchise laws. For decades, they focused on the sometimes conflicted challenges of building strong and loyal dealer networks and fighting dealer efforts to exploit their state law privileges to reduce retail competition and impose high costs on the manufacturers. From the 1930s through the second decade of the twenty-first century, automobile retail sales and service remained the exclusive province of franchised dealers, while the manufacturers confined themselves to designing and building cars. All of that would change dramatically when Elon Musk burst onto the scene with Tesla.

Notes

1. I owe this account of Whaling City Ford to my colleague Richard Primus, grandson of Sigmund and Rose.
2. D. N. Thompson, *Franchise Operations and Antitrust* (Lexington, MA: Heath Lexington Books, 1971), p. 20; Francine Lafontaine & Fiona Scott Morton, "Markets: State Franchise Laws, Dealer Terminations, and the Auto Crisis" (2010) 24 *Journal of Economic Perspectives* 233–50 at 234.
3. Thomas G. Marx, "The Development of the Franchise Distribution System in the U.S. Automobile Industry" (1985) 59 *The Business History Review* 465–74 at 465–66; *see also* Gary Michael Brown, "State Motor Vehicle Franchise Legislation: A Survey and Due Process Challenge to Board Composition" (1980) 33 *Vanderbilt Law Review* 385–440 at 387.
4. Kevin A. Wilson & Rusty Blackwell, "Sears Tried Twice to Sell Cars and Failed Miserably," Car & Driver, October 15, 2018, www.caranddriver.com/features/a23786730/sears-failed-selling-cars-twice/.

5. Thomas S. Dicke, *Franchising in America: The Development of a Business Method, 1840–1980* (Chapel Hill: University of North Carolina Press, 1992), p. 61.
6. Marx, "The Development of the Franchise Distribution System."
7. Ibid.
8. Brown, "State Motor Vehicle Franchise Legislation," p. 387.
9. Alfred P. Sloan, *My Years with General Motors* (Garden City, NY: Doubleday, 1963), p. 291.
10. Sloan, My Years with General Motors.
11. Ibid., p. 392.
12. Ibid.
13. Ibid., p. 395.
14. Ibid.
15. Stewart Macaulay, *Law and the Balance of Power: The Automobile Manufacturers and Their Dealers* (New York: Russell Sage Foundation, 1966), p. 10.
16. Ibid., p. 14.
17. *Encyclopedia of American Business History and Biography: The Automobile Industry 1920–1980* at 311 (1989).
18. Marx, "The Development of the Franchise Distribution System," p. 468.
19. Ibid., p. 468.
20. Ibid., p. 469.
21. Ibid.
22. Macaulay, Law and the Balance of Power, pp. 5–12.
23. Louis D. Brandeis, "A Curse of Bigness," Harper's Weekly, 10 January 1914, p. 18.
24. The NADA Story, "National Automobile Dealers Association," www.nada.org/nada/nada-story.
25. Higashiyama, *supra* note 3, at 4–5.
26. FTC, Report on Motor Vehicle Industry (1939).
27. Ibid., pp. 140–46.
28. Ibid., p. 174.
29. Ibid., p. 195.
30. Ibid., p. 202.
31. Ibid., p. 1076.
32. Ibid.
33. Ibid., pp. 365–418.
34. Sally H. Clarke, *Trust and Power: Consumers, the Modern Corporation, and the Making of the United States Automobile Market* (New York, NY: Cambridge University Press, 2007), p. 206.
35. 15 USC § 1222 (2012 & Supp. 2014); *Mitsubishi Motors Corp. v. Soler Chrysler-Plymouth, Inc.*, 473 U.S. 614 (1985); Automobile Dealers' Day in Court Act of 1956, Pub. L. No. 84-1026, 70 Stat. 1125.
36. Laws of Wisconsin, Ch. 378, Sec. 218.01(3)(a) (July 14, 1937).
37. *Forest Home Dodge, Inc. v. Karns*, 29 Wis 2d 78, 85 (1965).

38. Ibid.
39. Higashiyama, *supra* note 3, at 13.
40. Macaulay, Law and the Balance of Power, p. 32.
41. Ibid., p. 33.
42. Ibid., pp. 35–37.
43. Ibid., p. 11.
44. Ibid., p. 12.
45. Cynthia Barmore, "Tesla Unplugged: Automobile Franchise Laws and the Threat to the Electric Vehicle Market" (2014) 18 *Virginia Journal of Law & Technology* 185–228 at 189.
46. FTC Report, 311.
47. Dicke, Franchising in America, p. 69.
48. Ibid., p. 70.
49. Ibid., p. 202.
50. Mich. H. Legis. Analysis Section, Second Analysis, H.B. 4738, 4740, at 1 (1-26-99), www.legislature.mi.gov/documents/1997-1998/billanalysis/House/pdf/1997-HLA-4738-B.pdf.
51. Mich. H. Legis. Analysis Section, H.B. 5072 Synopsis (7-25-77).
52. *Ford Motor Co. v. Texas Dept. of Transp.*, 264 F 3d 493, 500 (5th Cir. 2001).
53. VA ST § 46.2-1572(3).
54. *Ford Motor Co. v. Texas Dept. of Transp.*, 264 F 3d 493, 500 (5th Cir. 2001).

2   ELON MUSK'S DIRECT SALES DECISION

In the early 2010s, Elon Musk surveyed the US car market. The visionary (and sometimes eccentric) South African entrepreneur was on his second wife and his third company, and he would go on to have plenty more of both. Musk had already made a fortune on the money transfer service PayPal, founded the rocket launch and space exploration company SpaceX, and then became the angel investor and CEO of Tesla, an electric vehicle (EV) start-up, in 2004. Tesla's first car, the Roadster, was the first street-legal, serially produced EV running on lithium-ion battery cells. The sleek Roadster attracted plenty of celebrity attention for Tesla, but it was hardly a competitor to Detroit. The car was essentially a prototype produced on the Lotus Elise chassis in the service bays of a former Chevy dealership. It cost over $100,000, and Tesla sold fewer than 2,500 units worldwide.

The Model S sedan, due to launch in 2012, was an entirely different proposition. Tesla built it from the ground up and produced it at a former General Motors (GM)/Toyota plant as its first mass-market offering.[1] Despite growing financial and production challenges, Musk was confident that he was making a product that consumers would find attractive. He would soon be vindicated when accolades for the Model S started pouring in. *Consumer Reports*, no easy grader, would go so far as to call the Model S "the best performing" car the magazine had ever tested.[2] Detroit started paying attention.

Musk had a great product to sell, but how would he get it to consumers? Among his pressing challenges was the question of how Teslas would be sold and serviced. As he surveyed the car market, Musk became convinced that Tesla could not succeed if it went the way of Detroit. The franchised dealer route that Sloan had endorsed in the 1920s would not work for an EV start-up a century later. Two historical precedents, one older and one newer, weighed on Musk's mind.

The first was the history of Detroit's relationship with the dealers. Over time, the dealer networks began to feel less like a competitive advantage and more like an albatross around the neck. The direct costs of maintaining a dealership network were immense. In the best of times, the state franchise dealer laws restricted a car company's ability to manage its dealerships efficiently. Underperforming dealerships were hard to cancel or to supplement with more competitive dealerships in the same geographic area. In the worst of times, the franchised dealer laws severely hampered a car company's ability to survive. For example, by the late 1990s, it had become apparent that GM had too many brands and that the historic Oldsmobile brand was a drain on the company. The first three letters – *Old* – said it all. GM's CEO, Rick Wagoner, reluctantly decided to cut the brand, but the franchise dealer laws made implementing that decision unexpectedly difficult and costly. GM had to pay its Oldsmobile dealers well over $1 billion just to terminate an unprofitable brand.[3]

To this first problem, one might respond that the Asian and European car companies had succeeded in playing by the conventional franchised dealer rules when they entered the US market in the 1970s and 1980s. But the successful entry of companies selling internal combustion engine vehicles could not answer a second, more recent precedent that weighed heavily on Musk's mind. Fisker Motors and Coda, both EV start-ups, had recently tried to enter the market and been driven to bankruptcy in short order.

Fisker was the brainchild of Danish car designer Henrik Fisker, who had been involved in the design of some of the world's most prestigious cars, including the Aston Martin DB9 and V8 Vantage and the BMW Z8. The company launched in 2007 with the Karma, one of the world's first plug-in hybrid vehicles. As with the Tesla Roadster, Fisker quickly attracted an A-list of celebrity owners, including Leonardo DiCaprio, Ashton Kutcher, Justin Bieber, Joe Jonas, Al Gore, Colin Powell, and Phil Mickelson. But, despite the glamour of its launch, Fisker stumbled into bankruptcy in 2013, leaving a glum Hollywood in its wake.

Coda Automotive, a less flashy EV start-up, unveiled its Pininfarina-designed prototype at the Beijing Auto Show in 2004. The EPA rated the vehicle's combined fuel economy at 73 miles per gallon, a seemingly attractive proposition for a world reeling from Middle Eastern wars and soaring oil prices. Yet, like Fisker, Coda went bankrupt in 2013, having sold only 177 cars.

Reflecting on Fisker and Coda's failures, Musk saw an important common denominator: Both companies had tried to sell and service their EVs through traditional franchised dealers, and both companies had failed.[4] To be sure, there was a lot more to the companies' failures than their distribution strategies. Fisker's litany of woes included multiple recalls of its batteries, production issues, managerial disputes, and, yes, a lawsuit in which Tesla accused Fisker of stealing its technology. (Fisker ultimately won the lawsuit, and Tesla was ordered to pay its legal fees.) And then there was the unfortunate fact that, in October 2013, Hurricane Sandy destroyed Fisker's entire European shipment of 338 Karmas at Port Newark, New Jersey. As to Coda, in contrast to the sex appeal of the Fisker Karma and Tesla Roadster, the Coda's bland design brought to mind the Yugo Commie-Car of the 1980s. But if Fisker and Coda's decision to sell through franchised dealers wasn't the sole cause of their demise, Musk was convinced that it was at least a significant contributing factor.

In October 2012, Musk – labeling himself Tesla's Chairman, Product Architect, and CEO – penned a blog post announcing "Tesla's approach to distributing and servicing cars."[5] Musk began by acknowledging that "it would be easier to pursue the traditional franchise dealership model, as we could save a lot of money on construction and gain widespread distribution overnight," and that "[m]any smart people have argued over the years that we should do this, just like every other manufacturer in the United States." So why was Musk insisting that Tesla take "a unique path?" Musk explained that "[e]xisting franchise dealers have a fundamental conflict of interest between selling gasoline cars, which constitute the vast majority of their business, and selling the new technology of electric cars."[6] He argued that "[i]t is impossible for [traditional dealers] to explain the advantages of going electric without simultaneously undermining their traditional business. This would leave the electric car without a fair opportunity to make its case to an unfamiliar public." Further, Tesla needed to be able to reach out to potential new customers proactively. "By the time most people decide to head to their local dealer, they have already pretty much decided what car they want to buy, which is usually the same make as their old car." But Tesla couldn't afford to wait for customers to seek them out – it had to take the message to customers by "positioning [its] store and gallery locations in high foot traffic, high visibility retail venues, like malls and shopping streets that people regularly visit in a relatively open-minded buying mood."

That was the affirmative case for Tesla's direct sales strategy. Musk then shifted to defense. Already, the company had faced two lawsuits challenging its direct sales model under the state franchise dealer laws, one by a Fisker dealer and the other by a dealer group in Boston demanding that it be granted a Tesla franchise. Musk responded with an argument that would become core to Tesla's legal position over the next decade:

> Automotive franchise laws were put in place decades ago to prevent a manufacturer from unfairly opening stores in direct competition with an *existing franchise dealer* that had already invested time, money and effort to open and promote their business. That would, of course, be wrong, but Tesla does not have this issue. We have granted no franchises anywhere in the world that will be harmed by us opening stores.

Musk's 2012 blog post laid out the blueprint for Tesla's direct sales rationale and gave company officials talking points on how to explain the importance of Tesla's distribution strategy for the company's ability to sell EVs. Over time, the company developed its arguments more systematically. In a January 19, 2016, workshop on automobile distribution convened by the Federal Trade Commission (in which I also participated), Todd Maron, Tesla's General Counsel, outlined seven reasons that the franchise dealer model wouldn't work for Tesla.[7]

First, Maron argued that "traditional dealerships are in large, out-of-the-way locations." That model wouldn't work for Tesla, which is why the company kept its stores small and placed them in high foot traffic areas like shopping malls. It was a matter of business common sense that when new technology comes out, "consumers don't go to it. You need to bring the new technology to the consumer."

Second, going back to the size point, Maron argued that traditional dealerships are large in size because they carry a lot of inventory. Inventory is the lifeblood of a traditional dealership – the sales commission model works based on the salesperson being able to get a browsing customer into a car that they can drive home. But Tesla didn't stock inventory in the same way as traditional internal combustion engine manufacturers. Its cars were custom-built for each individual customer, meaning they don't get built until they're ordered. Maron argued that this made selling Teslas unworkable for traditional franchise dealers.

Third, Maron argued that "the franchise dealer model is based on a high volume of fast-paced sales where customers come in already having done their shopping and knowing what they want. Salespeople are then paid by how quickly they can close the deal. The longer it takes, the worse it is for the salesperson, and the worse it is for the dealership." Tesla had to operate differently because it was selling a new product. Rather than convincing a customer to buy a known technology available on the lot, Tesla salespeople had to begin by educating potential customers on EV technology:

> They have many questions, questions about how to charge at home, how to charge away from home. What is range anxiety? How am I going to solve it? What are the incentives that are unique to EVs? What is the difference between the price of gas and electricity? How does the car actually work? What is regenerative breaking? What is dual motor?

Unlike customers buying a Ford or Honda, Tesla customers take a long time to study the car and EV technology. Although Maron did not quantify this in his testimony, I have been told by Tesla executives that the average customer interacts with Tesla about six times before deciding to make a purchase. It thus takes Tesla hours of patient education to close a deal. Franchised car dealers with salespeople working on commission would not have similar patience to educate customers on EVs. A commissioned salesperson who spent time educating a customer on a Tesla might be laying the groundwork for an eventual sale several interactions later with a different salesperson or at a different store.

Fourth, Maron argued that

> it is well known that franchise dealerships derive relatively little profit from new car sales. Instead, most all their profit comes from other parts of the house. Service and parts, trade and used car programs, financing products, insurance products, and other add-ons – we can't offer that to any franchised dealer, because we only profit in one way – from new car sales and new car sales alone.

Tesla couldn't make a profit from service because its cars have far fewer parts than internal combustion cars. There are no regular service visits for engine tune-ups and oil changes, since Teslas have neither engines nor oil. Tesla also doesn't make money off financing programs, insurance products, or add-ons. Maron argued that a "franchised dealer would look at this and just scratch their heads. They would not know how to make money in this model."

We can add some quantification to Maron's argument. Studies show that franchised dealerships earn much higher margins on servicing cars and selling add-ons compared to what they earn for selling new cars. A Forbes article by car analyst Jim Henry found that "[f]inancial results for the six publicly traded, new-car dealer groups in the United States show that to a great extent, dealerships are in the business of selling new and used cars so they can service them and finance them."[8] For example, for one dealer group, finance and insurance products represented only about 3 percent of their revenues but 20 percent of their gross profits. Selling service and parts was an even more important profit center:

> The Service and Parts Department is the real workhorse of dealership profits, representing both revenues and gross profit. For the Penske Automotive Group ... service and parts represented 13 percent of annual revenues, but 44 percent of the gross profits. The gross margin for service and parts was 57 percent for the Penske group, vs. just 8 percent for new-vehicle sales.

Given their economic profile, it would be surprising if dealerships found it attractive to sell Teslas, which promise little in the way of the service and parts revenues that fuel dealer profitability.

Fifth, Maron argued that "traditional dealerships rely on manufacturers to fund their advertising, which we see on TV, on the radio and on print media." But Tesla chooses not to advertise and certainly wouldn't allow, let alone subsidize, someone else to advertise for them. "What franchised dealer is going to accept not being able to advertise," Maron asked.

Maron's sixth point, which he identified as probably most important, was that franchised dealers could not make money selling Tesla because Tesla was committed to selling online and from company-owned stores wherever possible. So if Tesla was forced to franchise in one state but not an adjacent one or online, it would continue selling through company-owned stores in the adjacent state and online. The franchised dealer would have to mark up the Tesla to make a profit, but Tesla would continue selling at its regular prices in the adjacent state and online, which would induce customers to cross state lines to buy the car less expensively from Tesla. Maron was thus leaning into the exact argument that had fueled the direct sales bans in the first place. If a manufacturer opened its own retail stores, it could undermine the prices offered by its franchised dealers. Since Tesla clearly was going to be selling directly in some places – whether online or in friendly states – dealers would unavoidably face the exact "abuse" that had motivated the dealer franchise laws. Better not to have dealers at all.

Finally, like Musk earlier, Maron argued that dealers faced a conflict of interest with respect to EV sales. Unlike the dealers, Tesla was on a mission to save the planet: "We don't simply believe that EVs represent a nice complement to gas-powered cars. We believe it's imperative that they be replaced entirely by electric vehicles." However, "dealers are not fundamentally committed to the mission of EVs." Dealers "make 99% of their revenue off gas-powered cars. If you're opening a Yankees team store, are you going to ask a lifelong Red Sox fan to manage it? And what if he's still selling Red Sox gear out of another store down the road? Or, even worse, in the same store?"

Maron's argument that franchised car dealers show little commitment to selling EVs has gotten substantial support from consumer and environmental groups and investigative journalists. From December 2013 to March 2014, Consumer Reports sent nineteen secret shoppers to eighty-five dealerships in four states to determine how committed franchised dealers who did stock EVs (Chevrolet, Nissan, Honda, and Toyota – not Teslas, of course) were to selling them.[9] The secret shoppers asked questions designed to gauge how familiar the dealers were with EVs, whether they were just trying to sell whatever vehicles they happened to have on the lot, and whether they would recommend or discourage buying an EV. The results showed that "many dealership salespeople were not as knowledgeable about electric cars as you might expect." Consumer Reports found that "few provided accurate and specific answers about battery life and battery warranties. And many seemed not to have a good understanding of electric-car tax breaks and other incentives or of charging needs and costs." Overall, thirteen of the eighty-five dealers actively discouraged buying an EV and thirty-five recommended buying an internal combustion vehicle instead.

The Sierra Club has validated these findings through more recent studies. In 2019, it released a study "[b]ased on survey responses and testimonials from volunteers who called or visited 909 auto dealerships and stores across all 50 states."[10] Among other things, the Sierra Club found that 74 percent of dealerships were not selling EVs at all, "salespeople often failed to provide information on federal or state consumer incentives or were poorly informed or uninformative about EV technology," "10% of the time when volunteers asked to test drive an EV, the vehicle was insufficiently charged and unable to be driven," and "of the dealerships that sold EVs, more than 66% did not display EVs prominently, with vehicles sometimes buried far in the back." Things had not gotten much better when the Sierra Club took another look in 2023:[11] 66 percent of car dealers still did not have a single EV for sale, and 45 percent of those dealers "reported they would not offer an EV for sale regardless of automaker allocation and supply chain constraints."

There is little question that, not just when Musk first decided on a direct sales strategy but still a decade later, car dealers as a whole are not terribly interested in selling EVs. In 2023, Slate journalist Alexander Sammon visited the National Automobile Dealers Association annual convention and found that EVs were often the butt of jokes.[12] Given the economics of franchised dealer distribution, it is not surprising that dealers have little interest in turning to a technology that would displace their far more profitable sales of internal combustion vehicles.

Beyond dealer aversion to selling EVs, Tesla had another reason for deciding against partnering with franchised dealers that it did not mention in its public statements, but that occurred more and more to the company as it got deeper into its battles with the car dealers' lobby. Recall that in Chapter 1 we encountered Sloan's view that local dealers had a trust advantage over distant manufacturers. The dealer was "usually a substantial businessman in his local community" and could meet the customer "often as a neighbor." By the twenty-first century, however, the idea of the local car dealer as a trusted neighbor could only be the punch line of a joke. According to a 2024 KPA Dealership Trust Survey, conducted by The Harris Poll, consumer views on car dealers were overwhelmingly negative, with 76 percent of the respondents saying they did not trust dealerships to be honest about pricing, 86 percent concerned about hidden fees, and 84 percent reporting that price transparency is lacking at most car dealerships.[13] Another "34% have felt pressured to purchase 'add-ons,' 30% said they found hidden fees on the paperwork after they had agreed on a price, 28% felt a salesperson was trying to 'trick' them into a deal, and 29% left one dealership and went to another because they didn't think it was being honest in its pricing."[14] According to the Consumer Federation of America and Better Business Bureau, consumers complain about car dealerships more than any other business in the United States,[15] a remarkable feat given consumer antipathy to other loathed businesses like cable companies and debt collectors.

Here I will risk a little personal anecdotalism. Like many people, I have purchased a new car from a dealer on several occasions. While I have certainly encountered some fair and honest salespeople, that has been the exception rather than the rule. More often than not, the salesperson has tried to get me in the door by quoting an aggressive price for the vehicle and then tried to backfill the transaction with costly fees or extras that I did not request and made clear that I did not want. On one occasion, I had agreed with a Honda dealer on the purchase price for an Odyssey minivan. When my wife and I showed up for the closing, he informed us that the actual sales price would be over $1,000 more than we had previously agreed due to a small "clerical error." (My wife and I walked away.) When I went to buy a Subaru Outback instead, I found the final invoice loaded with fees and charges that hadn't been disclosed to me upfront. It took me several hours to get the invoice pared down to what we had agreed. Armed with these bad experiences, when I went to purchase a Subaru Forester some years later, I explained to the salesperson very clearly upfront that I did not want to show up to the closing to see any charges, fees, or extras on the invoice that we had not previously discussed. I explained that I would be happy to consider any extras so long as he told me about them now, I had time to research and think about them at home, and then I informed him before I came to the closing exactly what I did and didn't want, such that I understood to the penny the size of the check I had to write when I came to the closing. He swore to me in blood that this would be the case. When I came to the closing, the business manager presented me with an invoice loaded with a $1,200 service prepayment fee that I had already rejected. I wasn't one of the respondents to the Harris poll, but I know what they mean!

Stories like my own are unfortunately all too common. Frequently, people share their own similar car dealer stories. A few years ago, I was doing an interview for National Public Radio and my interviewer shared her own story about being charged $199 for VIN etching that she did not order and that turned out not even to have been done. To be fair, some people have good experiences with car dealerships too, but, as the Harris Poll and Better Business Bureau data show, the American public's honeymoon with the car dealers is long over.

Tesla had lots of reasons to decide to go it alone on selling and servicing its cars. Still, at least in the early years, Tesla did not rule out the possibility of eventually working with the dealers in some capacity. In 2013, Diarmuid O'Connell, Tesla's vice president for business development, told CNN that Tesla might consider working with dealers "in the future, when we're selling hundreds of thousands of vehicles."[16] In 2014, as Tesla's wars with the car dealers were getting underway, Elon Musk told *Autoline Daily* host John McElroy that Tesla might eventually need to consider "a hybrid system, with a combination of our own stores and some dealer franchises."[17] He may have had in mind the example of Apple, which briefly flirted with buying Tesla in 2015. Apple has long employed a dual distribution strategy, where it sells its products directly to consumers through its website or company-owned stores but also through third-party retailers such as Target and Best Buy or cellular providers such as AT&T and Verizon. As Tesla scaled up, maybe it would pursue a similar model.

Whatever Musk was thinking in the early years, the direct sales plan he launched in 2012 would remain the company's exclusive strategy for the next decade and beyond. And whatever interest Musk may have once had in rapprochement with the dealers quickly soured after the dealers' lobby launched their attacks on Tesla in legislatures, courthouses, governor's offices, and motor vehicle commissions across the country.

Tesla was the first, but certainly not the only, EV start-up to conclude that a direct sales approach was essential to its market penetration. Almost every other EV start-up has made the same decision, a list that includes Rivian, Lucid, Fisker, Faraday Future, Lordstown, Bollinger, Aptera, Nikola, Scout, and Arrival, among others. As we will see in Chapter 8, these companies had the simultaneous advantage and disadvantage of drafting in Tesla's wake. But, as a business matter, all made the same decision as Tesla: selling through franchised dealers would be unworkable.

The only EV start-up of which I'm aware that has decided to try its hand with franchised dealers is not a US company but Vietnam-based VinFast.[18] VinFast originally planned to go the direct distribution route, but says that in late 2023 it made "an important pivot from the capital-heavy, direct-to-consumer distribution model to a capital-light hybrid model with a strong focus on leveraging existing distribution infrastructure by building dealership networks in the U.S. and globally."[19] I'm interested to see whether VinFast ends up finding its dealer relationships "capital-light." The legacies certainly haven't. But let's not prejudge. If there's one point I'd like to leave the reader of this book, it's that there isn't a one-size-fits-all model of car distribution, that different companies have different needs and strategies, and that competition in the marketplace – not regulation – should decide which distribution models win or lose. I wish VinFast every success.

We will end this chapter with a coda about another EV start-up that tried dealer distribution – Fisker. After his flashy rollout and quick failure in the early 2000s, Henrik Fisker decided to try again in 2016. The new Fisker Inc. developed an ambitious plan for a new generation of EVs, including "an autonomous pod," a "solid-state battery-powered sports car," an "electric pickup truck," a "convertible grand tourer EV with up to 600 miles of range," a "fully connected mobility device" for young urban innovators, and even "the next Popemobile."[20] In 2023, the company released the Fisker Ocean, a sleek electric SUV. This time, Fisker abandoned its previous plans to sell through franchised dealers and, like every other EV start-up, went direct to consumers. Henrik Fisker observed that "we have entered into a whole new era of customer experience that evolved out of a smartphone," and that a direct sales model was necessary to reach a different generation of consumers.[21] Then, in January 2024, Fisker again shifted strategies and announced that it would pursue franchised dealers after all, having found direct sales too expensive and sales moving too slowly.[22] Maybe Fisker should have stuck with its direct sales strategy. By June 2024, Fisker had laid off most of its employees and again filed for bankruptcy.[23]

Fisker is not the only EV start-up to flash, flail, and then fail after trying (and, in Fisker's case, abandoning) a direct sales model of distribution. As we'll see in greater detail in Chapter 8, the British light commercial EV start-up Arrival and the Ohio-based Lordstown Motors suffered similar fates. And they surely won't be the last. Distribution is only one of many problems that an EV start-up has to solve. Fisker's attempted revival suffered from numerous system failures, including inadequate internal financial controls, running customer service using a Chatbot rather than a call center, failure to monitor component supplier problems, and legal problems over nonpayment of suppliers. As the history of the American car industry shows, starting a brand-new car company is no easy task, and most who try it will fail.

The direct sales model is not a panacea for struggling EV start-ups, nor for EVs to gain market acceptance more generally. But Elon Musk made a bet that, without a direct sales approach, Tesla had no chance of succeeding in the cutthroat automotive world. It soon became apparent that the biggest challenge to Tesla's distribution strategy would not be on the business or customer side, but in the realm of law and politics.

Notes

1. Elon Musk, "The Tesla Approach to Distributing and Servicing Cars," Tesla: Blog, October 22, 2012, www.tech-insider.org/electric-vehicles/research/2012/1022.html.
2. "Tesla Model S 2013–2015 Quick Drive," Consumer Reports, www.consumerreports.org/cro/video-hub/cars/hybrids--alternative-fuel/tesla-model-s-20132015-quick-drive/14786539001/2366240882001 (last visited Nov. 14, 2015).
3. Paul Ingrassia, *Crash Course: The American Automobile Industry's Road from Glory to Disaster* (New York: Random House, 2010), p. 67.
4. Ben Popper, "Auto Dealers Fire Back at Tesla CEO: 'This Musk Guy, He Wants All the Profits for Himself,'" The Verge, March 19, 2014, www.theverge.com/2014/3/19/5525544/new-jersey-auto-dealers-respond-to-teslas-elon-musk.
5. Elon Musk, "The Tesla Approach to Distributing and Servicing Cars," Tesla: Blog, October 22, 2012, www.tech-insider.org/electric-vehicles/research/2012/1022.html.
6. Ibid.
7. "Auto Distribution: Current Issues and Future Trends," Workshop Hosted by the Federal Trade Commission, January 19, 2016, www.ftc.gov/system/files/documents/public_events/895193/auto_distribution_transcript.pdf.
8. Jim Henry, "The Surprising Ways Car Dealers Make the Most Money Off You," Forbes, February 29, 2012, www.forbes.com/sites/jimhenry/2012/02/29/the-surprising-ways-car-dealers-make-the-most-money-off-of-you/.
9. Eric Evarts, "Dealers Not Always Plugged in About Electric Cars, Consumer Reports' Study Reveals," Consumer Reports, April 22, 2014, www.consumerreports.org/cro/news/2014/04/dealers-not-always-plugged-in-about-electric-cars-secret-shopper-study-reveals/index.htm.
10. Hieu Le & Andrew Linhardt, "A Nationwide Survey of the Electric Vehicle Shopping Experience," Sierra Club, November 2019, www.sierraclub.org/sites/default/files/program/documents/2153%20Rev%20Up%20Report%202019_3_web.pdf.
11. Larisa Manescu, "Sierra Club Releases Nationwide Investigation into Electric Vehicle Shopping Experience," Sierra Club, May 8, 2023, www.sierraclub.org/press-releases/2023/05/sierra-club-releases-nationwide-investigation-electric-vehicle-shopping.
12. Alexander Sammon, "Want to Stare Into the Republican Soul in 2023?," Slate, May 30, 2023, https://slate.com/news-and-politics/2023/05/rich-republicans-party-car-dealers-2024-desantis.html.
13. "Survey Shows Consumers Have Little Trust in Dealerships," Auto Remarketing, March 5, 2024, www.autoremarketing.com/ar/retail/survey-shows-consumers-have-little-trust-in-dealerships/#:~:text=The%20perception%20of%20dealerships%20among,lacking%20at%20most%20car%20dealerships.

14. Ibid.
15. "2013 – Nation's Top Ten Consumer Complaints," Consumer Federation of America, July 30, 2014, https://consumerfed.org/press_release/nations-top-ten-consumer-complaints-3/.
16. Peter Valdes-Dapena, "Tesla's Fight with America's Car Dealers," CNN, May 20, 2013, https://money.cnn.com/2013/05/20/autos/telsa-car-dealers/index.html.
17. Sebastian Blanco, "Elon Musk Hints at Need for Franchised Tesla Dealerships," Autoblog, October 15, 2014, www.autoblog.com/2014/10/15/elon-musk-hints-at-need-for-franchised-tesla-dealerships.
18. "VinFast Officially Signs Agreements with 12 New Dealers in the US," VinFast, April 23, 2024, https://vinfastauto.us/investor-relations/news/vinfast-officially-signs-agreements-with-12-new-dealers-in-the-us.
19. Ibid.
20. Sean O'Kane, "Inside EV Startup Fisker's Collapse: How the Company Crumbled under Its Founders' Whims," TechCrunch, May 31, 2014, https://techcrunch.com/2024/05/31/fisker-collapse-investigation-ev-ocean-suv-henrik-geeta/.
21. Tamara Chuang, "Electric-Vehicle Makers Want to Sell Directly to Coloradans, Dealers Say That's a 'Solution in Search of a Problem'," The Colorado Sun, February 17, 2020, https://coloradosun.com/2020/02/17/electric-vehicle-makers-direct-sales-colorado-bill/.
22. Sean McLain, "EV Startup Fisker Ditches Tesla-Style Direct Sales Model," The Wall Street Journal, January 4, 2024, www.wsj.com/business/autos/fisker-ditches-tesla-style-direct-sales-model-in-favor-of-dealerships-31dd71c0.
23. Sean McLain, "Electric-Vehicle Startup Fisker Files for Bankruptcy," The Wall Street Journal, June 18, 2024, www.wsj.com/business/autos/electric-vehicle-startup-fisker-files-for-bankruptcy-0a3eb7d6.

3   THE EMPIRE STRIKES BACK

Jim Appleton had a job on his hands. For almost twenty years, he had served as the President of the New Jersey Coalition of Automotive Retailers (typically known as NJ Car), the lobby representing New Jersey's 520 car dealerships.[1] A lawyer by training, Appleton worked as intergovernmental relations director for the New Jersey Department of Environmental Protection and for a government relations firm before joining NJ Car in 1997. His NJ Car job was to protect the interests of New Jersey's car dealers. Usually, that meant fighting one of two forces – consumer advocates that wanted to pass laws more strictly regulating car dealers or car manufacturers like General Motors (GM) and Ford that wanted more leeway in managing their franchised dealers. In March 2014, Appleton met a brand-new foe in the form of Elon Musk.

In 2013, Tesla had quietly applied to the New Jersey Motor Vehicle Commission ("NJMVC") for two licenses to operate retail stores in New Jersey. The Commission, apparently not seeing the coming storm, granted the licenses. Within a few months, Tesla had opened its stores and sold 500 cars. When NJ Car got wind of it, the proverbial poop hit the fan. Publicly, Appleton claimed that the Commission had "goofed."[2] One suspects that stronger language may have been used behind closed doors. In any event, under pressure from NJ Car and with the backing of Republican governor Chris Christie, the Commission moved to enact a new rule to make sure that neither Tesla nor any other car company could ever sell its cars in the state.

My own story intersected with Mr. Appleton's on March 12, 2014, when we were thrust into a debate on Bloomberg television. A few weeks earlier, I had only a vague idea about the state franchise dealer laws. I had taught antitrust and contract law for years, but was unaware that most states prohibited a car manufacturer from selling its own cars to consumers. Then I read a news story about the situation brewing in New Jersey and NJ Car's arguments for why Tesla shouldn't be allowed to sell direct. I read the article, blinked once or twice, and then read it again thinking I must have missed something. I hadn't. The dealer arguments for banning direct sales were flatly contrary to uncontroversial economic principles that had been well understood for a very long time. I wrote a blog post pointing out some of the historical and economic fallacies of New Jersey's direct sales ban and then suddenly found myself debating Mr. Appleton on Bloomberg.

Jim was close to New York and appeared in person in Bloomberg's studio. I appeared remotely from a University of Michigan studio in Ann Arbor. As I quickly learned, an in-person debater has a big advantage over a remote one. Appleton got to say about three words for each of mine. And what he said left my head spinning. He started by arguing that New Jersey law prohibited Tesla from selling directly to consumers and that Tesla just had to play by the rules. The obvious problem with this argument was that the NJMVC had granted Tesla's dealer applications in the ordinary course of business and then turned around and passed a new regulation banning direct sales once the dealers screamed. He then argued that Tesla was a "monopoly," and so it was unfair for Tesla to sell its own cars. A monopoly, really? Tesla's market share was less than 1 percent. Where I come from in antitrust law, that's not called a monopoly. But the clincher was Appleton's final argument: In this country we regulate even cats and dogs, he argued, so Tesla needed to accept being regulated too.

As discussed in greater detail in Chapter 4, the argument that Tesla was somehow trying to escape being regulated is a red herring. Tesla had applied for a dealers' license *so that it could be regulated as any other car dealer in New Jersey*. The irony of Appleton's argument was that, once Tesla was banned from opening stores in New Jersey, it could continue selling cars to thousands of New Jersey residents over the Internet or in other states without being regulated in New Jersey. But that is really a quibble with his argument. The far more surprising point is his assertion that because we accept regulation of one thing – dogs and cats – we just have to grin and bear regulation of another, entirely unrelated thing. As we'll see, the dealers' arguments against Tesla have not gotten much more sophisticated than that.

In his usual inimitable style, Elon Musk wasted little time in upping the rhetorical ante with the person at the top – in this case Governor Christie. In a March 14, 2014, blog post "To the People of New Jersey,"[3] Musk stated that "under pressure from the New Jersey auto dealer lobby to protect its monopoly, the New Jersey Motor Vehicle Commission, composed of political appointees of the Governor, ended your right to purchase vehicles at a manufacturer store within the state." Noting that the NJMVC had justified the direct sales ban as necessary to "consumer protection," Musk threw down the gauntlet: "If you believe this, Gov. Christie has a bridge closure to sell you." That was a nonsubtle reference to the scandal involving the September 2013 closure of the George Washington Bridge, which was allegedly instigated by Christie aides for political reasons. Reveling in New Jersey pop culture, Musk then flung out a Sopranos reference, arguing that Christie and the NJMVC were offering "a mafia version of 'protection.'" So much for "a soft answer turns away wrath!"

Jim Appleton also upped the verbal ante, asserting that Musk was "an Internet billionaire" who thinks the world revolves around him and that "the world springs from [his] laptop."[4] But Musk's boisterous strategy may have worked. A year later, Christie signed into law a statute that allowed Tesla to open up to four dealerships in New Jersey. Now it was NJ Car's turn to complain that the new legislation allowed Tesla to maintain "a vertical monopoly and eliminate[] competition."[5] (At least it was now clear what Appleton meant by Tesla having a "monopoly".)

The skirmishing between NJ Car and Tesla would continue for years. In 2018, after Tesla opened stores in Springfield, Cherry Hill, Paramus, and the Short Hills Mall, NJMVC cited Tesla for illegally opening a fifth store at Garden State Plaza. Tesla responded that it had opened a "gallery" rather than a store, and the matter settled. Displeased with the state's supposedly overly lenient treatment of Tesla, NJ Car filed a lawsuit accusing the New Jersey Division of Consumer Affairs of failing to enforce consumer laws regarding alleged violations of advertising regulations by Tesla, such as accepting deposits for a $35,000 Model 3 car and then selling it at a higher price.⁶ The court dismissed the dealers' complaint for lack of standing in 2021, a pattern that would be seen elsewhere in the country.

New Jersey was just one battleground in many state-level battles between Tesla and the car dealers that began around 2014. As noted in Chapter 1, the state dealer laws passed in the mid twentieth century varied considerably from state to state, so the legal, regulatory, and political arguments available to the dealers varied by state. In some states, most importantly California, the dealers had no good argument that existing state law prohibited direct sales, since the law only prohibited a manufacturer that actually had franchised dealers from opening a retail location in competition with its existing dealers. In many states, however, either the existing law arguably applied to Tesla, or it could be made to do so with some legislative tweaking or regulatory manipulation. Thus, in states such as New York, Massachusetts, and Missouri, the dealers brought lawsuits to block Tesla from opening stores, arguing that direct sales were illegal under existing law. In states such as Michigan, West Virginia, and Arkansas, the dealers lobbied the legislature to adopt new laws that would explicitly ban direct sales. And, in states such as Georgia, Virginia, Kentucky, and Wisconsin, the dealers fought Tesla's petition to the motor vehicle commission for the right to open stores in the state. At the same time, Tesla was on the legislative offensive in states such as Ohio, Washington, New Hampshire, Utah, Vermont, and Wyoming where it secured carveouts that allowed it to operate at least some stores in the state.

Later chapters will report on some of these state-by-state battles in greater detail and also on the overall landscape today. For now, let's more closely examine the legal issue that doomed NJ Car's lawsuit, because it provides a good window into the significant shift that occurred between the passage of the dealer protection laws in the mid twentieth century and the crop of anti-Tesla litigation in the early twenty-first century. There is no better way to examine that issue than through the lens of the challenge the dealers brought against Tesla in Massachusetts.

In 2013, Tesla's Massachusetts subsidiary opened a gallery at the Natick Mall, ten miles west of Boston. The Massachusetts State Auto Dealers Association ("MSADA") immediately brought a lawsuit alleging that the gallery was "the functional equivalent of a dealership showroom, intended to generate sales of Tesla vehicles" and that this was prohibited under the state's franchised dealer statute.[7] Tesla initially proclaimed its innocence, arguing that a gallery was not a sales center and therefore not covered under the law. Things changed a few months later when the Natick Board of Selectmen approved Tesla's application to open an actual store. There was now no question that Tesla was planning to sell Teslas in Massachusetts, and the car dealers weren't happy about it. (Interestingly, one of the dealers that joined the lawsuit was a Fisker dealership, which presumably had nothing better to do in light of Fisker's bankruptcy.) Tesla now shifted legal gears and argued that the dealers lacked standing to bring their challenge. The trial judge agreed with Tesla and dismissed the dealers' complaint, sending the case to the Massachusetts Supreme Judicial Court.

Massachusetts' highest court sided with Tesla. Much of its opinion is a technical parsing of the relevant Massachusetts statutes, but the court also made a core point that applies generally to the direct sales issue. The court noted that the purpose of Massachusetts' direct sales prohibition "historically was to protect motor vehicle dealers from a host of unfair acts and practices historically directed at them by their own brand manufacturers and distributors."[8] The law's legislative history showed that the legislature's purpose was to prevent car manufacturers from competing unfairly with their own franchisees, not to prevent competition from a car manufacturer from a different brand. The dealers argued that they would be injured by Tesla's direct sales model because Tesla would be able to thwart the considerable costs that other dealerships would spend to conform to Massachusetts law, and that this would lead to "inequitable pricing" and "consumer confusion."[9] However, the court held, "the type of competitive injury they describe between unaffiliated entities is not within the statute's area of concern."[10] In economic parlance, the Massachusetts statute was designed to limit *intra*brand competition, not *inter*brand competition, therefore the dealers lacked standing to pursue a theory premised on interbrand competitive harm.

There is much to say about the dealers' argument about how they were harmed by competition from Tesla's direct sales model. As we will see in Chapter 4, the dealers have frequently argued that direct sales are bad for consumers because, by eliminating intrabrand retail competition among different dealers in the same brand, direct sales lead to higher consumer prices. But the Massachusetts dealers admitted just the opposite. Their entire theory was that Tesla could save money through direct sales, which it would pass on to consumers in the form of lower retail prices, which would competitively injure the dealers who were forced to charge higher prices because of their franchise model. Accusing Tesla of causing competitive injury through "inequitable prices" only makes sense if Tesla could charge lower prices than the dealers. If direct sales caused Tesla to charge higher prices, the dealers would have nothing to complain about.

The Massachusetts court did not consider the merits of the dealers' argument that direct sales lead to inequitably low prices. Like New York and Missouri courts that reached the same result,[11] it held that the dealers lacked standing to challenge Tesla because the law was meant to protect dealers in an existing franchise relationship with a manufacturer, not to limit competition from a manufacturer that did not employ dealers at all.

Although these decisions are technically about standing, they also encapsulate the very important shift that took place between the passage of the dealer franchise laws and Tesla's arrival. As we saw in Chapter 1, the dealer franchise laws arose out of a historical context in which dealers were family-owned mom-and-pops beholden to the power of the Big Three. The inequality of bargaining power between manufacturer and franchisee and abuses within contractual franchise relationships were the motivating force behind the state direct sales prohibitions. There were no examples of companies like Tesla pursuing pure direct sales strategies, nor was there any discussion about potential effects on consumers of such strategies. Therefore, whatever the technical language of the various state statutes, the use to which the dealers were trying to put those statutes – blocking interbrand competition from a vertically integrated manufacturer – was no part of the statutes' history or rationale.

The dealers realized that they could not get traction against Tesla by going back to the original dealer protection purposes and history of the franchise dealer laws. For the reasons cited by the various courts denying them standing, those rationales had no application to Tesla. But the dealers also faced a more fundamental historical problem: The business and economic circumstances of the mid twentieth-century automobile market had radically changed in the intervening years, as had the political culture around protecting small business. Arguments for dealer protection were no longer viable in the twenty-first century.

Recall that the central thrust of the dealers' successful argument for protection in the mid twentieth century was that there was a gross disparity in bargaining power between the car manufacturers, which were large and powerful oligopolists, and the car dealers, which were mom-and-pop businesses. By 2014, neither of those contentions would pass the laugh test.

First, the US car market had gone from an oligopoly dominated by three manufacturers to an unconcentrated market with the participation of many different automotive groups. In addition to GM, Ford, and Chrysler, car dealers could now choose to partner with Toyota, Honda, Nissan, Hyundai-Kia, Subaru, Volkswagen-Audi, Mazda, Mitsubishi, BMW, Mercedes, Volvo, Jaguar, and many other smaller foreign companies selling in the US market. The fact of much more competition at the manufacturer level increased the dealers' bargaining power and allowed them to better protect themselves in contractual negotiations.

But an even more striking change had occurred on the dealer side. Most dealers were no longer mom-and-pops, but very large – often gigantic – multi-state conglomerate groups comprising scores or even hundreds of dealerships under the same corporate roof. In 2013, four dealership groups – AutoNation, Penske Automotive Group, Sonic Automotive, and Group 1 Automotive – made the Fortune 500. In 2012, the thirty-three largest dealership groups each had over $1 billion in revenue.[12] The ten largest dealership groups had combined annual revenue of over $80 billion, more than the GDP of many countries. Even the 100th largest dealership group had annual revenues over $300 million. By 2016, the top ten dealership groups had revenues exceeding $100 billion,[13] and six dealership groups had annual revenues exceeding Tesla's. In my home state of Michigan, the largest dealership group, the Suburban Collection, operated forty-seven new car dealerships and ten additional auto-related service centers in Michigan and had $2.3 billion in revenue in 2016.[14] The largest non-Michigan-based dealer group operating in Michigan, the Ken Garff

Automotive Group, operated three dealerships in Michigan out of the fifty-five total dealerships it operated and had over $4.3 billion in revenue in 2016.

Those businesses are hardly mom-and-pops, but maybe there are still lots of mom-and-pop dealerships out there in need of legal protection. Let's take a look at the National Automobile Dealers Association's own figures. According to NADA's 2023 Annual Financial Profile of America's Franchised New-Car Dealers,[15] there were 16,835 new light-vehicle dealerships in the United States. (This is different from the total number of franchises, since many dealerships operate with multiple brand franchises.) All together, these dealerships earned $1.2 trillion in revenue, with an average of $71,710,000 per dealership. But many dealerships were part of larger ownership groups. In 2014, 95 percent of dealers were part of ownership groups owning 1–5 dealerships, but this number had fallen to 91.6 percent by 2023. Meanwhile, all other ownership group categories (6–10, 11–25, 26–50, and over 50) grew over the same period. Thus, over the first decade of the Tesla wars, there was a clear trend toward consolidation among the car dealers.

Nonetheless, most dealers remain in groups of 1–5, meaning that their average group revenues are somewhere between $72 million and $360 million. Could they still lay a claim to being "small businesses?" The Small Business Administration ("SBA") uses two different measures – revenues and number of employees – to define a small business. For new car dealers, it uses the number of employees rather than revenues.[16] For used car dealers, its cutoff is $40 million, so most new car dealers would lose out. But the SBA defines new car dealerships as small businesses if they employ fewer than 200 employees. According to NADA data, the average dealership has sixty-three employees, but the SBA accounts affiliate dealerships for determining whether a dealership is a small business.[17] So the average car dealership in a group of three or fewer dealerships might just squeak under the SBA cutoff, but most will not. In other words, most car dealerships are no longer small businesses even under the SBA's generous definitions. With average revenues per dealer of $72 million, most aggregated into larger dealership groups, and most hitting hundreds of millions or billions of dollars in revenues, it would be farcical to continue describing most dealers as "mom-and-pop" businesses.

In combination, the much greater competitiveness of the car manufacturing market and the tremendous growth of the dealer groups would call into serious doubt an ongoing claim that the dealers needed to be "protected" from the manufacturers. Tellingly, that original rationale for the direct distribution bans almost never cropped up during the Tesla wars. Instead, as we have already seen in New Jersey and Massachusetts, the car dealers turned to a consumer protection argument to protect themselves from direct sales competition. That argument will be debunked in Chapter 4. For now, it is worth asking the following question about the car dealers: Given the complete change in economic and business circumstances since the passage of the franchise dealer laws, how did the dealers manage to maintain their privileged position against manufacturer competition for so long? After all, as discussed in Chapter 2, car dealers were no longer the belles of the ball in the eyes of the American public. And, when polled about whether Tesla should be able to sell its cars directly to consumers, the American public – including 99 percent of respondents in an LA Times poll according to Elon Musk – overwhelmingly said that it should.[18]

The simple answer is that car dealers wield a lot of political power. The roughly 18,000 dealerships employ about 1.2 million people. And dealers are spread across the country and within states. In the industry, there's a saying that "there's a dealer in every district." Whether or not the dealers remain trusted as beacons of their communities as Sloan thought in the 1920s and 30s, they are certainly important economic and political presences at the local level. The dealers are politically well organized at the national level through NADA and at the state and local levels through groups like NJ Car and MSADA. They give lots of money in state, local, and federal elections and lobby aggressively for their interests. Open Secrets reports that "historically, car dealers have devoted more resources to political contributions than domestic automakers themselves," with about 70 percent of contributions going to Republican candidates and 30 percent to Democrats.[19] (More on this interesting fact in Chapter 7.) In the 2014 election cycle, NADA alone disbursed over $2.9 million in campaign contributions, not to mention the resources it spent on lobbying activities.[20]

Not only do the dealers give lots of money to politicians but many of them also get elected to office themselves. In 2024, Congressman

Roger Williams (R-Texas), who chairs the House Small Business Committee, led the charge against the Biden Administration's electric vehicle (EV) policies, alleging that "the EV market is phony."[21] In addition to chairing the House Small Business Committee, Congressman Williams chairs Chrysler Dodge Jeep RAM SRT in Weatherford, Texas.[22] He has been joined in Congress by Rep. Mike Kelly (R-Pa.) and Rep. Vern Buchanan (R-Fl.), both of whom also own dealerships.[23] They face a possible counterweight across the aisle in Rep. Don Beyer (D-Va.), also a former dealer, but will get reinforcement from Bernie Moreno, the Trump-endorsed Republican who won election to the Senate from Ohio in 2024 and who is the president of the Collection Auto Group, a car dealer company. Up and down state legislatures also, dealers or people closely associated with dealers wield political clout (as we shall see in Chapter 6 with respect to the Michigan story).

The dealers' activism and political strength are only one part of the explanation for how the dealers have managed to hold onto the franchise dealer laws long after their original justification has faded. Two other forces have kept a steady wind blowing at the dealers' backs. The first is the power of incumbency. The American political system is conservative in the sense that it is designed to make legal and political change difficult. It typically takes a majority or even supermajority in two legislative chambers, the signature of a chief executive, and the acquiescence of the courts for legal changes to take effect. The car dealers began the Tesla wars with the law on the books in their favor – or at least arguably so in many states. The dealers were therefore in a pole position to argue for preserving what had been in place for decades, whereas Tesla often had to argue for change. Even though it would have been difficult for the car dealers to secure brand-new legislation prohibiting direct sales in most states, it was a much lighter lift to defend their existing turf.

The second source of wind at the dealers' backs is what is described in public choice theory as the asymmetrical distribution of benefits and harms between producers and consumers. In most states, there are a few hundred car dealers and millions of consumers who buy cars and need to have them serviced. If the franchise dealer laws do what MASDA admitted they do – allow the dealers to charge higher prices than if they faced competition from direct sales – then the dealers will have a concentrated interest in preserving the monopoly rents protected by those laws. A few hundred dealers – many of whom are part of the same dealer groups – will not find it difficult to band together and raise the resources needed to mount a political fight against legal reform (or even to lobby for the more challenging ask of new legislation). By contrast, the price paid by consumers is spread thinly across millions of people. While the aggregate cost to consumers may be very high, no individual consumer loses more than a few hundred dollars over her lifetime. Meanwhile, each car dealer (or dealership group) would lose millions of dollars if the system changed. Mobilizing millions of consumers to fight for reform is much more challenging than mobilizing a few hundred dealers to resist it.

To make this idea tangible, take as an example Mississippi's 2023 direct sales ban, described in Chapter 9. According to NADA data, there are 175 dealerships in the Magnolia State,[24] some of which share common ownership. Coordinating that small a number of companies through the Mississippi Automobile Dealers Association should be a relatively easy task. By contrast, there are over 2.3 million personal motor vehicles registered in Mississippi.[25] That's a lot of consumers to motivate and coordinate. Most people who buy a new car do so just a few times in their lives, so the rules governing automobile sales aren't high on their minds most of the time. Even if Mississippians as a whole pay a high price for the state's direct sales ban, most individual Mississippians have bigger fish to fry in their daily lives. Meanwhile, selling cars *is* the dealers' daily lives, and they make protecting their livelihood their daily business.

Add to this that the direct sales issue is not simple to explain. People get confused about where the franchise dealer laws came from historically, why EV start-ups need direct sales to survive, and why the dealers are wrong in claiming that allowing direct sales will increase prices. On more than one occasion, I've done a radio interview in which the host was sympathetic to Tesla's position but struggled to understand the issues even after ten or fifteen minutes. (Maybe that's on me!). The car dealers' lobby has done its best to foster that confusion with soundbites. Tesla just needs to follow the law. Tesla is a monopolist. Dogs and cats!

The Empire Strikes Back

To be sure, not every car dealer has opposed Tesla's right to sell directly to the public. A few have broken ranks and publicly stated that the EV start-ups should be allowed to do what they want and that direct sales are not a threat to traditional franchised dealers. AutoNation CEO Mike Jackson made waves in 2014 when he called Michigan's ban on direct sales (discussed in Chapter 6) "unnecessary protectionism."[26] Jackson correctly interpreted the history of the franchise dealer laws as being about relationships between franchising manufacturers and their franchisees, not interbrand competition. Further, Jackson showed the courage of his convictions that direct sales was a bad *business* strategy for Tesla: "If Elon Musk wants to make a mistake and go with an inefficient distribution system," he told the audience at the Detroit Economic Club, "that's his right as an American." He added that AutoNation wasn't afraid of Tesla's direct sales model and predicted that his "phone will ring someday when he really wants to sell some cars."

Unfortunately, Jackson's approach has been an outlier among the car dealers and their lobby. The vast majority of dealers don't seem to think that Tesla's direct sales approach is a bad business strategy. Like MSADA, they think it's a far too *good* one – one that will eat their lunches. Nothing else can explain the vast resources the car dealers have poured into fighting Tesla on a state-by-state basis. In Chapter 4, we will examine their arguments for why Tesla and other car companies should be prohibited from selling and servicing their own cars.

Notes

1. "Laura Perrotta to Lead NJ CAR as Jim Appleton Steps Down," New Jersey Coalition of Automotive Retailers, August 7, 2024, www.njcar.org/latest-news/laura-perrotta-to-lead-nj-car-as-jim-appleton-steps-down/.
2. Aaron Smith, "Tesla Lashes Out at Chris Christie," CNN Business, March 11, 2014, https://money.cnn.com/2014/03/11/news/companies/tesla-new-jersey/index.html.
3. Danielle Wiener-Bronner, "Elon Musk Takes His Fight Right to Chris Christie," The Atlantic, March 14, 2014, www.theatlantic.com/business/archive/2014/03/teslas-elon-musk-fires-back-christie-over-ban/359198/.
4. Ben Popper, "In Major Reversal, New Jersey Allows Tesla to Sell Its Cars Directly, without Dealerships," The Verge, March 18, 2015, www.theverge.com/2015/3/18/8251821/tesla-new-jersey-direct-sales-dealerships-christie.

5. Ibid.
6. David P. Willis, "NJ Gives Tesla Special Treatment, and that Hurts Consumers, Car Dealers Say," app., September 20, 2019, www.app.com/story/money/business/consumer/press-on-your-side/2019/09/20/nj-tesla-car-dealers-lawsuit/2373245001/.
7. *Massachusetts State Automobile Dealers Association, Inc. v. Tesla Motors MA, Inc.*, 469 Mass 675, 678 (2014).
8. Ibid., pp. 684–85.
9. Ibid., p. 684.
10. Ibid.
11. *Greater New York Automobile Dealers Association v. Department of Motor Vehicles*, 969 NYS 2d 721, 882 (N.Y. Sup. Ct. 2013).
12. WardsAuto 2013 Dealer 500, WardsAuto, May 29, 2013, www.wardsauto.com/software-defined-vehicles/wardsauto-2013-dealer-500; *State ex rel. Missouri Automobile Dealers Association v. Missouri Department of Revenue*, 541 SW 3d 585 (Mo. Ct. App. 2017).
13. "2016 Top 150 Dealership Groups," Automative News, March 26, 2017, www.autonews.com/article/20170327/DATACENTER/170329873/.
14. Daniel A. Crane, "The Fiction of Locally Owned Mom and Pop Car Dealers: Some Data on Franchised Automobile Distribution in the State of Michigan" (2017) *University of Michigan Law & Economics Research Paper Series*.
15. "2023 Annual Financial Profile of America's Franchised New-Car Dealerships," NADA Data, www.nada.org/media/4695/download?inline.
16. "Table of Small Business Size Standards Matched to North American Industry Classification System Codes," US Small Business Administration, www.sba.gov/sites/default/files/2023-06/Table%20of%20Size%20Standards_Effective%20March%2017%2C%202023%20%282%29.pdf.
17. "2023 Annual Financial Profile of America's Franchised New-Car Dealerships," NADA Data, www.nada.org/media/4695/download?inline.
18. Danielle Wiener-Bronner, "Elon Musk Takes His Fight Right to Chris Christie," The Atlantic, March 14, 2014, www.theatlantic.com/business/archive/2014/03/teslas-elon-musk-fires-back-christie-over-ban/359198/.
19. "Car Dealers Summary," Open Secrets, www.opensecrets.org/industries//indus?ind=t2300.
20. Ibid.
21. Timothy Cama, "What Do Car Dealers in Congress Think of EVs?," Politico, June 4, 2024, www.eenews.net/articles/what-do-car-dealers-in-congress-think-of-evs/.
22. John Dunbar, "Congressman-auto Dealer Accused of Conflict of Interest," The Center for Public Integrity, November 18, 2015, https://publicintegrity.org/politics/congressman-auto-dealer-accused-of-conflict-of-interest/.
23. *What do car dealers in Congress think of EVs?*, Politico (June 6, 2024), www.eenews.net/articles/what-do-car-dealers-in-congress-think-of-evs/.

24. "2023 Annual Financial Profile of America's Franchised New-Car Dealerships," NADA Data, www.nada.org/media/4695/download?inline.
25. "2023 Light-Duty Vehicle Registration Counts by State and Fuel Type," US Department of Energy, https://afdc.energy.gov/vehicle-registration.
26. John Voelcker, "Michigan Anti-Tesla Law 'Unnecessary Protectionism': AutoNation CEO," Yahoo!, November 10, 2014, https://autos.yahoo.com/michigan-anti-tesla-law-unnecessary-protectionism-autonation-ceo-160823844.html.

4   IT'S THE CONSUMER, STUPID!

Rosemary Shahan had had enough. It was 1979, and the thirty-two-year-old Ms. Shahan had brought her car into a San Diego car dealership for what she thought would be minor repairs.[1] To her growing frustration, the car sat at the dealership for three months with nothing happening. Fed up with the nonsense, Shahan began picketing daily outside the dealership. So was born a lifelong crusade on behalf of automobile consumers. She went on to become one of the country's leading consumer advocates, playing a major role in the passage of California's lemon laws, spearheading consumer protections against unsafe, predatory, and discriminatory practices in the automobile industry, and founding Consumers for Auto Reliability and Safety ("CARS"), a leading consumer advocacy group.

The automobile industry isn't for the fainthearted. In her decades of fighting to protect consumer rights in legislatures across the country, Shahan had to grow a thick skin. But she never lost sight of the people for whom she was fighting. Ralph Nader once described Shahan as "tenacious as a bulldog, consistent as the Milky Way, and as humane in her own way as Mother Teresa"[2]

When Tesla's wars against the car dealers began, Shahan went all-in on a manufacturer's right to sell direct to the consumers. She gave me a long list of reasons: "Dealers make a lot of their profits from selling financing and worthless add-ons that hike up the cost of buying and financing cars at dealerships by tens of billions of dollars;" "new and used car dealers are the most-complained-about businesses in America;" "dealers engage in many illegal activities, such as odometer tampering, salvage fraud, rebuilt wreck fraud, falsifying loan applications, and other scams that harm consumers;" and "dealers engage in identity theft." To Rosemary Shahan, the direct sales issue isn't so much about Tesla's right to decide on its own distribution arrangements; it's about *consumers'* rights to decide for themselves how to buy their own cars.

Shahan and CARS have been at the center of a major shift in the regulation of automobile distribution. The franchise dealer laws adopted in the mid twentieth century were solely animated by protecting dealers from competition by their own franchising manufacturers. Consumer interests were hardly part of the story at all. But, as we saw in Chapter 3, by the time of Tesla's entry in the second decade of the twenty-first century, dealer protection arguments were no longer viable, certainly at least as to companies that did not employ franchised dealers at all. The dealers therefore invented a new rationale for the prohibitions on direct sales: They were in place to protect *consumers* from the manufacturers. Rosemary Shahan has had a lot to say about that.

In this chapter, we will see what's wrong with the dealers' arguments. But before getting into the merits, it's worth noting that the dealers have a serious credibility argument in advancing a consumer protection argument. It's not just that, as we saw in Chapter 2, franchised car dealers have a terrible PR problem with the American public. More fundamentally, if prohibiting direct sales really was about protecting consumers, one would expect various organizations that exist to protect consumers to rally to the dealers' cause. But exactly the opposite has happened. Not a single consumer organization has taken the dealers' side. To the contrary, not just Rosemary Shahan and CARS but also the Consumer Federation of America and Consumer Action have taken the position that direct sales bans harm consumers and that companies like Tesla should be allowed to determine their own distribution strategy. So too has EVHybridNoire, an organization that exists to find "creative human/community-centric data-driven, equitable programs that deliver innovative solutions."[3]

What about governmental agencies that protect consumer interests? In 2015, the senior staff of the Federal Trade Commission (FTC) – the Directors of the Office of Policy Planning, the Bureau of Competition, and the Bureau of Economics – were asked by a

Michigan legislator to offer their view on direct sales.[4] Writing in support of legislation that would permit direct sales, the FTC staff made a number of comments sharply contrary to the car dealers' self-serving assertions about consumer protection. They wrote that a "blanket prohibition on manufacturer sales to consumers is an anomaly within the larger economy," that "when manufacturers respond to competitive pressure by choosing to vertically integrate, consumers usually benefit through lower prices and/or higher quality," and "[i]n contrast, when the government intervenes and outlaws vertical integration, consumers often experience worse service and higher prices." In sum, the "FTC staff believe that current law, interpreted to ban direct manufacturer sales of motor vehicles, is very likely anticompetitive and harmful to consumers."

The dealers' consumer protection arguments are contradicted by consumer protection organizations and the federal agency charged with protecting consumers. They also have no support from economists or other academics who study competition, vertical integration, or consumer protection. To the contrary, I have organized a number of open letters, policy papers, *amicus curiae* (friend of the court) briefs, and op-eds that have been joined by hundreds of economists and law professors who specialize in these topics and represent the spectrum of political ideology from right to left. These have included many former top antitrust officials at the FTC and Justice Department and a Nobel laureate in economics. All argue that the dealers' arguments are flatly wrong. And, unlike most policy issues with which I've been involved as an academic, there isn't a group of academics on the other side. On several occasions when these issues were going to be discussed at conferences, I diligently looked for academics to take the other side and never found anyone.

But maybe the dealers are nonetheless on to something. To get into the merits of the dealers' arguments, let's start with a point made in the FTC letter: "FTC staff offer no opinion on whether automobile distribution through independent dealerships is superior or inferior to direct distribution by manufacturers. Rather, staff's principal observation is that consumers are the ones best situated to choose for themselves both the vehicles they want to buy and how they want to buy them." The important point here is that there is no general view in economics about whether one method of distribution is more advantageous than another. In a market unconstrained by regulation, manufacturers will employ the distribution strategy that optimizes their ability to make profits. For example, Gateway, Compaq, and Dell Computers traditionally sold their products directly to consumers. (Dell started selling both direct to consumers and through independent retailers in 2008.)[5] By contrast, most other computer companies sold primarily through independent retailers. Apple pursued a mixed model, selling both directly and through third-party retailers. Nothing in economic theory says that any of these models is likely to be better as a general matter than any other. Instead, competition between different companies will determine which models work the best in which circumstances.

The dealers have made a great point of arguing that Tesla's direct sales strategy will not work as a business model. At the 2016 FTC hearings discussed in Chapter 3, a consultant for the car dealers spoke at length about how Tesla was making a terrible *business* mistake in thinking that it could sell directly to consumers. We already saw the answer to that objection, given by the CEO of AutoNation, in Chapter 3. If a company chooses an inefficient distribution strategy, it will be punished in the market and either have to change strategies or go out of business. There is no need for a law prohibiting bad business strategies.

Nonetheless, throughout the Tesla wars, there has been fierce contestation over an issue that only experimentation and competition can decide – whether Elon Musk (and now the rest of the electric vehicle (EV) start-ups) are actually right in arguing that direct sales is their best distribution strategy and whether it actually produces savings to consumers. The dealers naturally put a lot of energy into contesting reports that direct sales save consumers money. One such episode made national news in 2015.

In 2009, an economist at the US Justice Department published a paper on the Justice Department's website suggesting that direct sales could save consumers up to 8 percent on the purchase of new automobiles.[6] The report relied primarily on a 2000 Goldman Sachs study, which quantified potential cost savings based on improvement in matching supply with consumer demand, lower inventory costs, fewer dealerships, lower sales commissions, and lower overall shipping costs.

The report also noted that General Motors (GM) had been selling direct to consumers on a build-to-order model in Brazil for the previous eight years and that an auto analyst had opined that this could result in "spectacular improvements in the company's competitiveness and profitability."

After the Justice Department report was cited in some advocacy pieces about direct sales (including my own), I received an email from the Media and Public Relations Director for NADA forwarding a link to a blog post by Glenn Kessler, a Washington Post blogger who runs a well-known "Fact Checker" blog. Kessler's post argued that the Justice Department report was "bizarrely outdated."[7] Kessler pointed out that GM had discontinued its direct sales approach after six years because it wasn't working, so any claims about the success of direct sales must be incorrect.

There were several notably suspect aspects to Kessler's "fact checking" (beyond the unanswered question of who had put him up to it – surely not NADA!). For one, the claims about GM's success with direct sales in Brazil were hardly the central thrust of the DOJ report; the Goldman study featured much more prominently. But even more suspect was that, according to Kessler's own blog, GM had decided to stop direct sales in Brazil after six years based on two factors: One was "the infrastructure costs to maintain distribution centers." That one could plausibly have undermined arguments about the efficiency of direct sales. But the other factor was "federal and state tax changes in the country" and the "wildly complicated" Brazilian tax code, including an obligation of paying a value added tax based on the location of the merchant rather than the location of the customer. For all the information available to Kessler, the predominant factor that killed GM's direct sales strategy in Brazil may have been a tax change that disadvantaged direct sales, not anything inherent in the economics of the model. Another example of bad regulation! At a minimum, the evidence Kessler cited was sufficiently ambiguous on the reasons that GM stopped direct sales in Brazil, and GM in Brazil was so not the main thrust of the DOJ's analysis, that one had to wonder why a prominent fact checker for a major national media outlet bothered with it at all.

The obvious answer is that the dealers were desperate to undermine any claim that direct sales is actually a viable and efficient distribution model. Of course, the only real way to find out what effect direct sales would have on Tesla's business success would be to stop armchair speculation and let direct sales happen. The dealers wouldn't need the force of law to coerce Tesla into pursuing a more efficient business model, nor would they be alarmed if it pursued an inefficient one. The only argument that could possibly make sense for why *legal* regulation is needed is that a manufacturer might pursue a distribution strategy that maximized the manufacturer's profits but harmed consumers. The dealers' consumer protection arguments rise or fall on such evidence.

In Chapter 3, we saw the crude form of the dealers' argument – that Tesla is a "vertical monopoly." Let's now bring in some dealer voice to flesh that out. Texas Auto Dealer Association President Bill Wolters has argued that "to me fewer dealers drives the price up.... The price doesn't go down when they have fewer outlets. And when they talk about the manufacturer being able to save more selling direct, there's nothing that says they pass that along to the customer."[8] Jonathan Collegio of NADA argued that Tesla "would not have the same set of incentives to keep costs down that dealers have, because they would not have competitors within the same brand. (For example, two Chevy stores owned by GM can't really compete with each other in the same way as two business owners with skin in the game.)"[9] Similarly, NADA spokesman Charles Cyrill argued that "for consumers buying a new car today, the fierce competition between local dealers in any given market drives down prices both in and across brands.... If a factory owned all of its stores, it could set prices and buyers would lose virtually all bargaining power."[10]

These arguments aren't expressed in formal economic terms, but to examine them more closely, let's do that work for them. All of these assertions boil down to the allegation that a company that is vertically integrated into distributing its own products will set a higher retail price than would be offered to consumers if the company allowed independent dealers to compete to sell its products. That assumption is simply erroneous as a matter of economics.

To be sure, in some circumstances a manufacturer's products can be sold less expensively if they are sold by independent retailers than by the manufacturer. Take Heinz ketchup, for example. When was the last time you bought ketchup in a Heinz store? Of course you haven't, because Heinz doesn't open stores to sell its products, but instead relies on supermarkets to do so. There is a simple economic reason for this. Consumers almost never go out shopping for just ketchup; they shop for baskets of grocery products. It is therefore much more efficient for ketchup and other grocery products to be sold by grocery stores than by the companies that make those products. No law had to tell Heinz not to open its own stores. If it did, it would pretty quickly go out of business.

So, yes, direct sales to consumers *sometimes* make no *business sense* because independent retailers have superior economies of scale or scope in distribution. If dealer distribution turns out to be more efficient than direct sales, Tesla and other EV manufacturers will eventually gravitate toward dealers – in their own self-interest. But observe that this is an entirely different phenomenon than the car dealers' claim about Tesla. Their argument is that Tesla has *an incentive* to jack up retail prices of its own cars to monopoly levels in order to earn higher profits, whereas car dealers facing competition from other car dealers would be forced to offer competitive prices. That argument is bunk.

To see why, think about two different manufacturers. One operates in a highly competitive market. If it raised its prices above competitive levels, it would lose most of its sales and go out of business. That would be true whether it sold to retailers at wholesale or sold directly to consumers at retail. Either way, the manufacturer would be constrained by competition and could not raise prices to consumers.

Now consider the other manufacturer, which has some market power in its brand. Consumers are willing to pay a premium price for its products, and it charges a high wholesale price to retailers. Suppose a light bulb goes off in some executive's brain: We can make even more money by opening up our own retail stores and charging an additional monopoly mark-up at retail. That executive would shortly be fired, because the idea of charging one monopoly mark-up at wholesale and then a second monopoly mark-up at retail in order to increase profits is economic malpractice. The monopoly mark-up at wholesale already represented the maximum profit that the manufacturer could take from its brand. A further monopoly mark-up at retail would effectively diminish the manufacturer's wholesale sales and the manufacturer's profits, because consumers would buy less of the manufacturer's product.

This economic principle – called "double marginalization" – has been widely recognized since 1838 when it was demonstrated by a French mathematician named Augustin Cournot. Cournot showed that when two companies with market power at separate levels of a vertical chain (i.e., a manufacturer and a retailer) apply a monopoly mark-up to their prices, the price to the end consumer will exceed the price that a single company would charge if it controlled both levels of the vertical chain. Vertical integration can therefore lead to lower consumer prices, even if it results in no efficiencies other than the elimination of double marginalization. (To be sure, vertical mergers can also have anticompetitive effects in some circumstances – consult the Justice Department and FTC's merger guidelines if you're interested – but none of those are relevant to the debate over manufacturers opening their own dealerships.)

The upshot is that the claim that Tesla would be tempted to add a monopoly mark-up to its retail price on top of whatever monopoly mark-up it could charge at wholesale has been known to be wrong for nearly 200 years. The dealers who have made this argument – including some that have cross-examined me during legal proceedings – have mistaken a separate issue. The dealers have pointed out that intrabrand competition – competition between dealers in the same brand – can lower retail prices. That is undoubtedly true in the limited circumstance where a manufacturer decides to sell through independent franchised dealers, and some of them may have market power. If a retailer with market power adds a monopoly mark-up to the retail price, not only will consumers suffer but so also will the manufacturer since consumers will buy fewer of its products at retail, which in turn will lead to fewer wholesale orders. Thus, as the Supreme Court has recognized for many decades, the interests of manufacturers and consumers are aligned on not wanting retailers to exercise market power.[11] Intrabrand competition is beneficial in preventing the exercise of retailer market power, but that in no way means that a manufacturer can increase its profits by eliminating its franchisees and charging a monopoly mark-up at retail. As previously explained, that would lower, not increase, the manufacturer's profits.

The dealers' price argument doesn't pass the economic laugh test. A variation in their argument is even worse. As noted in Chapter 2, part of Tesla's direct sales strategy is to charge a single, flat, non-negotiable price. Elon Musk has famously threatened Tesla employees who try to give customers discounts, even insisting that his seventy-five-year-old mother has to pay full price.[12] The dealers have cited this as evidence that Tesla's refusal to allow dealers to sell its products is jacking up prices. After all, customers are losing the benefit of haggling with dealers to secure lower prices.

It takes a special lack of self-awareness for the dealers to flaunt haggling with pearly-teeth salesmen with well-coiffed hair as a great virtue of the American republic. Given the data on consumer experiences with car dealers reported in Chapter 2, it seems likely that the average car buyer would be willing to pay a premium *not* to have to bargain with commissioned car dealers. Jack Gillis of the Consumer Federation of America has debunked the dealers' argument, stating that most consumers prefer *not* to have to haggle over prices.[13] At Tesla stores, there is no haggling over price or high-pressure sales tactics to close a deal. In fact, business analysts fault Tesla employees for being *too passive* in trying to close sales, likening them to "museum curators" rather than salespeople.[14] In any event, there is no good reason to think that the elimination of haggling over prices will lead to higher prices to consumers. The function of a haggling sales model is not to lower average prices to consumers but to *lead to different prices to different consumers* based on the consumers' different willingness to pay (or what economists call their demand elasticity or reservation prices). Think of the difference between haggling at a bazaar or shopping at Target. At the bazaar, some consumers manage to get great deals, while others get fleeced. At Target, no one gets a great deal but also no one gets fleeced. Nothing in economic theory predicts that, as a general matter, the average price paid by consumers will be higher or lower in one circumstance or the other.

Although the dealers are wrong in claiming that the elimination of bargaining means that consumers pay higher prices overall, their argument about haggling does point to one important issue of equity. By eliminating haggling, Tesla (and other EV start-ups) mitigated a well-documented tendency of haggling with car dealers to result

It's the Consumer, Stupid! 61

in inequitable outcomes along racial and gender lines. As shown in several studies by Yale economist Ian Ayres,[15] women and African Americans pay much higher prices than white males when forced to haggle over car prices. Ayres had 38 testers, including 5 black males, 7 black females, and 8 white females, negotiate for over 400 automobiles, including 9 car models at 242 dealerships. He found that, compared to white males, "black males clearly fared the worst, paying an extra $962 over white males on initial offers and $1132 on final offers." Black females fared second-worst, being offered a final price that was $446 higher than that offered to white males. White females did comparatively better, being offered a final price $215 higher than that offered to white males.

Ayres' results are hardly unique. A 2018 study by the National Fair Housing Alliance found that minorities shopping for cars at dealers were offered far inferior loan terms and would have paid on average $2,662 more over the life of the loan.[16] A 2023 study by the Federal Reserve Bank of Chicago found that "strong evidence of racial and ethnic discrimination when auto financing is arranged through auto dealers…. This disparity in rates results in Black, Hispanic, and Asian borrowers often paying hundreds – or sometimes even thousands – of extra dollars in loan payments relative to their White counterparts."[17]

To be sure, racial and gender discrimination in car buying is a complex phenomenon and won't go away entirely with a flat, one-size-fits-all pricing model for new cars. Nonetheless, by eliminating haggling, the flat price model takes a big step forward toward reducing racial and gender disparities. The dealers are wrong that the model will likely lead to higher consumer prices, and even if the net price effects of the flat price model were neutral, there could be important positive social effects in reducing the incidence of discrimination.

In addition to asserting that direct sales will eliminate price competition and increase consumer prices, the dealers make several other consumer protection arguments. One set of claims has it that if manufacturers open their own stores, they won't provide adequate service for their customers. One flavor of this argument insists that manufacturers would provide poor warranty service. For example, Florida Automobile Dealers Association ("FADA") lobbyist Dave Rambo has argued that "[t]he new car dealer is the customer's advocate when it comes to warranty work and service on a manufacturer's product," and "[t]he attempt by auto manufacturers to cut out the dealer would only result in higher prices and less customer service to the public."[18] Other dealers' lobbyists have argued that honoring warranties is a cost to the manufacturer but a profit center to the car dealers, so car dealers can be better trusted to make sure that warranties are honored.

Beyond the fact that the dealers cite no evidence of car companies systematically refusing to honor their warranties, there are several reasons to think that this argument is make-weight. First, car companies have legal obligations to honor their warranties. Warranties are contractual obligations and, in addition, are regulated by the federal Magnuson-Moss Act, which the FTC enforces. But probably more importantly, car companies would suffer reputational harms if they developed a practice of refusing to honor their warranties. Over the last several decades, car warranties have become a salient selling point. Hyundai has long advertised itself as offering "America's best warranty," and consumer-oriented publications rate and rank the car companies' warranty coverage. (In 2024, U.S. News & World Report listed Tesla, Rivian, and Lucid in its "13 New Car Brands with the Best Warranty Coverage.")[19] Consumers (not to mention the FTC and class action lawyers) would punish companies that developed reputations for refusing to honor their warranties.

The dealers' warranty argument does raise an important consumer interest point, but it goes against the dealers' argument. Recall from Chapter 2 that car dealers make most of their money off of service – earning gross margins of up to a hefty 57 percent. How can the dealers make so much money off of service? A big part of the answer goes to a different feature of state franchise dealer laws – provisions governing warranty reimbursement and providing detailed formulas for the rates that manufacturers have to pay dealers for doing warranty work. The effect of these laws is to require manufacturers to reimburse dealers at rates that far exceed the dealers' costs and are not subject to competition. University of Florida economist David Sappington studied four car manufacturers accounting for a bit less than 50 percent of car sales in Florida between 2008 and 2012 and found that the increased cost to those manufacturers of the warranty service law was $80 million.[20] Many states have laws prohibiting a manufacturer from imposing a surcharge based on the cost of warranty reimbursement, but that doesn't mean that consumers don't pay. Instead, it means that car companies will calculate the inflated costs of paying for warranty service as part of their cost of doing business and include that in the price of new cars. Guess who pays for that.

Car companies like Tesla that don't use franchised dealers don't have to worry about paying inflated warranty reimbursement rates since they do that work themselves. That, in turn, should translate into savings to consumers.

One of the ironies about the warranty argument is that the dealers are trying to use the franchise dealer laws *to prevent* Tesla and other EV manufacturers from establishing or maintaining service centers that could provide warranty service. For instance, as this book goes to press, litigation is ongoing over the Louisiana Motor Vehicle Commission's ("LMVC") order purporting to shut down Tesla's sole service center in Louisiana. Tesla argues that it *wants* and *needs* to provide service in the state, especially so it can honor its legal obligations with respect to warranties. It has alleged the Louisiana Automobile Dealers Association effectively controls the LMVC and was behind the effort to boot Tesla's service center. Nine of the LMVC's fifteen commissioners are car dealers.[21] Whether or not the dealers are ultimately proved to be responsible for the LMVC's order, at minimum the franchise dealer laws are being used to prevent customers from getting access to warranty coverage rather than making sure the manufacturers honor their obligations.

Another variant of the dealers' argument about service goes like this (according to the Texas Automobile Dealers Association): "If Tesla were to go out of business, the service centers will, too. How, then will Tesla cars get needed repairs and maintenance? And what if there's a recall?"[22] The obvious problem with this argument is that if a manufacturer goes out of business, its dealers won't stay in business either. After Fisker went bankrupt the first time, there was no deep pocket to pay for warranty reimbursement, sell parts, or provide new cars, and its franchised dealers didn't stick around. But that doesn't mean that Fisker owners were completely stranded. While Fisker franchised dealers were no longer around to help, third-party repair companies stepped up to fill the void.[23] To be sure, a car company's bankruptcy leaves its customers in a lurch, but mandating sales and service through franchised dealers does nothing to mitigate that problem.

Two more dealer "consumer protection" arguments have even less merit and can be given a quick back of the hand. The first argument is that car sales are pervasively regulated and that dealer distribution is necessary in order to ensure compliance with state regulatory requirements, such as titling, registration, and lemon law protection.[24] To the extent that the dealers mean that direct sales results in the manufacturer not being required to meet these same regulations, their argument is perverse for reasons already explained. The EV manufacturers are seeking to be licensed as dealers *so that they are subject to these regulations*. The dealers may mean something different – that they are more to be trusted to comply with regulatory requirements than manufacturers. That argument has no empirical or theoretical basis and also seems a bit rich coming from the most-complained-about business in America. Moreover, the dealers should worry about the implications of their argument. If comparative rates of compliance with the law should dictate whether manufacturers or dealers get to sell cars, then compliance rates could be put to an empirical test. If the dealers get the short end of that stick, their own argument suggests that states should *close down all of the dealerships and require direct sales for everyone.*

The second argument, made by NADA, is that dealers are the consumer's champions on safety recalls.[25] Dealer lobbyists point to scandals involving GM's failure to issue timely safety recalls, leading to a number of deaths, as a reason that the manufacturers cannot be trusted on recalls. But, inconveniently for the dealers, the GM recall failures all occurred in the context of franchised distribution. So if the dealership model is supposed to serve as a guarantor of vehicle safety, then the GM recall failures are failures of the dealership model, not reasons to require it. In any event, dealers do not make recall decisions. Under federal law, the obligation to report vehicle safety defects to the National Highway Traffic Safety Administration ("NHTSA") rests solely on the manufacturer. The submitting manufacturer then proposes a remedial program, which is reviewed for approval by the NHTSA. If manufacturers fail to implement recalls requested by NHTSA, the agency may issue an administrative order requiring a recall. This entire process is run by the manufacturers and the NHTSA without dealer involvement. The dealers have also argued that, once a recall is issued, the dealers have a greater incentive to see it performed than do the manufacturers, since the manufacturer is paying the dealer to perform the service. But this argument assumes that, having issued an NHTSA-mandated recall, a manufacturer-owned service center will refuse to perform the service when customers request it. That would be a flagrant and easily detectable violation of federal law, and there is no reason to think it would be a systematic problem.

None of the dealers' consumer protection arguments have any merit. If they did, they would surely be taken up by consumer advocacy groups, but those groups have come out *against* the dealers. When push comes to shove – and particularly when exercising their significant lobbying clout with wavering elected officials – the dealers and their allies typically turn to another argument, one not based in consumer protection. They argue that independent franchised dealers are economically and philanthropically important to their states and local communities, and that killing off dealers will harm tax revenues, employment, local business opportunity, and even the Boy Scouts.[26]

The first thing to note about this argument is the assumption that allowing direct sales will kill off the car dealers. In this book's final chapter, we will see that the franchised car dealer model does indeed face some existential threats, but that direct sales is not high on that list. If the car dealers are correct that direct sales is a poor business strategy, then allowing direct sales should hardly threaten their existence.

While the dealers frequently claim that direct sales will kill jobs, nothing of the sort has happened over the last decade despite Tesla selling millions of cars without dealers. According to the Bureau of Labor Statistics ("BLS"), in January 2014, there were 1,163,000 people employed by automobile dealers.[27] A decade later, after Tesla and other EV start-ups had entered the market and rapidly grown their market share, car dealer employment had grown by 131,000–1,294,000. Nor has this resulted in car dealer employees earning less. In January 2014, the average hourly wage of production and nonsupervisory employees employed by car dealers was $19.71.[28] A decade later, it had grown to $27.63. According to the BLS's inflation calculator, that wage increase exceeded inflation.[29] In other words, over the decade that Tesla broke into the market, the number of car dealer employees increased and they were paid more.

Moreover, even if some independent franchised dealers are replaced by manufacturer-owned stores, that hardly translates into either a loss of "localism," economic activity, or tax revenues. As previously noted, most car dealers are hardly locally owned businesses anymore. Further, as with other dealer arguments, one of the ironies of the dealers' argument is that their lobbying is preventing new economic investment in their states. Tesla and other EV manufacturers are able to sell over the Internet regardless of any state's franchise dealer laws. What the EV start-ups are trying to do is open local brick-and-mortar stores in the states – stores that will employ local people, make local economic investments, and pay state and local taxes. The dealers are trying to block that from happening.

States that block Tesla or other EV manufacturers from establishing physical stores risk losing economically to other states that do allow direct sales. Thousands of consumers from every state are buying Teslas whether or not there's a local Tesla store. If they buy the car out of state or over the Internet, they have to pay a sales tax in the state in which they bought it or to which Tesla attributes the sale for purposes of its business license. When the customer brings the car back to his or her home state, they have to pay a sales tax again to register their car, but typically get credit for whatever sales tax they paid to the other state. Some states have reciprocity agreements where the state in which the sale was made rebates the tax to the home state – but many do not. A state that has no reciprocity agreement with the selling state and grants a tax credit to its residents ends up losing a significant amount of tax revenue. In 2021, I calculated the effect in my home state of Michigan. Annual sales taxes on cars account for $1 billion, about 10 percent of Michigan's tax revenues. Michigan does not have tax reciprocity agreements with about a quarter of the states. If Michigan lost sales tax revenues in proportion to the number of states without reciprocity agreements, and EV direct sales hit a 10 percent market share, that would mean a loss of $25 million in tax revenues. At 40 percent EV market penetration, the number would grow to $100 million in lost tax revenues. Michigan could gain back those lost revenues simply by allowing EV manufacturers to sell to Michigan residents under a Michigan dealer's license.

What about the argument that dealers are important philanthropies in their local communities? There is no doubt that many car dealerships make worthy contributions to local charitable causes. But do they do so more than other businesses? The dealers have produced no evidence that they do. According to the dealers' own self-survey, fewer than half of the dealers donated more than $25,000 to nonprofit organizations or charitable causes in 2013.[30] As a matter of policy, one should ask whether it makes sense to grant the dealers a monopoly on distribution in the hopes that they will voluntarily share some of their profits to subsidize worthy public causes. At a minimum, a law protecting the franchise dealer model based on the dealers' charitable virtues should rest on empirical evidence, not the dealers' self-serving say-so.

None of the arguments presented in favor of banning EV direct sales holds much water. I want to add in one more argument that I've never heard squarely made, but about which there are hints in some of the advocacy of scholars associated with a movement called Law and Political Economy ("LPE"), which was influential in the Biden Administration. The LPE movement argues that economic power is too heavily concentrated in America today, and that one important function of law and regulation is to diffuse economic power in society. In this hypothetical argument, laws that prohibit manufacturers from selling and servicing their own products require them to spread out some of the power in the manufacturer's brand to other companies – the dealers. By fracturing the manufacturer's economic power, the franchise dealer laws help to create multiple, offsetting centers of economic influence. And that in turn promotes democracy by preventing too much power from remaining concentrated in any single set of hands.

On other issues, I have written sympathetically to claims that the overconcentration of economic power tends to undermine democracy, but any such argument would be off to the market as to car distribution. As we've seen, economic power in the car manufacturer market has already become quite diffuse by virtue of foreign entry. It's becoming even more diffuse by the wave of new EV entry, including by American companies such as Tesla and Rivian. If anything, the dealer laws created entry barriers to more competition – and hence obstacles to more diffusion of power – in the market. A few years ago, I received a call from a representative of a major foreign car company that does not do much business in the United States. Speaking on the condition of anonymity, they informed me that the company was interested in entering the US market, but had concluded that the cost of establishing a dealer network was prohibitive. If they were allowed a more flexible distribution strategy – selling their own cars through a combination of online sales, full-service showrooms, and mall kiosks – they would be a lot more interested in making a go of it. I regrettably had to inform them about the challenges of direct sales given the still-evolving legal and political landscape.

As we've seen, it's also not the case that most of the dealers are small businesses anymore. Redistributing economic power from car manufacturers to multi-billion dollar Fortune 500 companies in order to save democracy doesn't make much sense. A much better plan is to level the playing field so that different car companies and dealers can experiment with different distribution strategies that meet their needs and satisfy their customers. And the ultimate decentralization of power is to allow consumers the choice of how they buy their cars. Telling consumers that they have no choice but to haggle with car dealers does not seem like the kind of line Thomas Jefferson would have added to the Declaration of Independence.

In sum, there is no merit to the dealers' arguments against direct sales, whether grounded in consumer protection or dealer protection, nor is there any other good argument for why a company should be prohibited from selling its own products to consumers. As we close this chapter, it is worth repeating a point made throughout this book: While, for the reasons explored in Chapter 2, there are good reasons to think that direct sales are vital to an EV start-up's ability to survive and to EV market penetration more generally, the case for direct sales does not depend on proving that point. In a market-oriented economy, there is only one way to find out whether a particular business strategy works or doesn't: by testing it in a competitive market. The burden on the car dealers is to show that the direct sales experiment is so likely to fail that it shouldn't even be allowed. Not a single consumer advocacy group believes the dealers have met that burden.

It's the Consumer, Stupid!   69

The case for allowing EV start-ups like Tesla to pursue a direct sales model is strong. But what about the legacy car companies like GM, Ford, Chrysler, and their foreign competitors? As we will see in Chapter 5, that story is just as interesting.

Notes

1. "Oral History Interview with Rosemary Shahan on December 06, 2007," MediaSpace at Central Connecticut State University, October 3, 2018, https://mediaspace.ccsu.edu/media/Oral+history+interview+with+Rosemary+Shahan+on+2007+Dec.+06/1_vxvhz0jc/149975081.
2. "About C.A.R.S.," CARS, www.carconsumers.org/about.htm (last visited February 15, 2025).
3. "About Us," EVNoire, www.evnoire.com/about-us (last visited February 15, 2025).
4. Letter from the Federal Trade Commission's Office of Policy Planning, Bureau of Competition, and Bureau of Economics to Michigan Senator Darwin R. Booher, May 7, 2015, www.ftc.gov/system/files/documents/advocacy_documents/ftc-staff-comment-regarding-michigan-senate-bill-268-which-would-create-limited-exception-current/150511michiganautocycle.pdf.
5. Lionel Mechaca, "Dell Focuses on Selling Products Direct and Through Retail," January 20, 2008, www.dell.com/en-us/blog/dell-focuses-on-selling-products-direct-and-through-retail/.
6. Gerald R. Bodish, "Economic Effects of State Bans on Direct Manufacturer Sales to Car Buyers" (2009) Economic Analysis Group Competition Advocacy Paper 1–13 at 4, www.justice.gov/atr/economic-effects-state-bans-direct-manufacturer-sales-car-buyers.
7. Glenn Kessler, "Key Report in Battle Over Car Dealer Sales Is Bizarrely Outdated," The Washington Post, February 24, 2015, www.washingtonpost.com/news/fact-checker/wp/2015/02/24/key-report-in-battle-over-car-dealer-sales-is-bizarrely-outdated/.
8. Jeff Cobb, "Why Tesla Is Opposed by Auto Dealer Associations," GM-Volt, May 22, 2013, www.gm-volt.com/threads/why-tesla-is-opposed-by-auto-dealer-associations.337189/.
9. "Should Tesla (And Other Auto Manufacturers) Be Able to Sell Cars Directly To Consumers?," Our Energy Policy, October 23, 2014, www.ourenergypolicy.org/should-tesla-and-other-auto-manufacturers-be-able-to-sell-cars-directly-to-consumers/#comments.
10. Michael Martinez & Michael Wayland, "Snyder Weighs Pulling Plug on Direct Tesla Sales," Detroit News, October 16, 2014, www.detroitnews.com/story/business/autos/2014/10/16/tesla-faces-direct-sales-ban-michigan/17359253.

11. *Leegin Creative Leather Products v. PSKS, Inc.*, 551 US 877, 896 (2007) ("[T]he interests of manufacturers and consumers are aligned with respect to retailer profit margins."); *Continental T.V., Inc. v. GTE Sylvania Inc.*, 433 US 36, 56 (1977) (noting that manufacturers would like to minimize the cost of distribution – the difference between the wholesale and retail price).
12. Jeanine Mancini, "Elon Musk Doesn't Give Family, Including His 75-Year-Old Mother, Early Access or Discounts on Teslas, Saying, 'The Price You See Is the Family Discount'," Yahoo! Finance, March 5, 2024, https://finance.yahoo.com/news/elon-musk-doesnt-family-including-164309722.html.
13. Peter Valdes-Dapena, "Tesla's Fight with America's Car Dealers," CNN, May 20, 2013, https://money.cnn.com/2013/05/20/autos/telsa-car-dealers.
14. Steve Finaly, "Mystery Shoppers Put Tesla Dealerships in Cellar – Again," Wards Auto, July 10, 2016, www.wardsauto.com/tesla/mystery-shoppers-put-tesla-dealerships-in-cellar-again.
15. Ian Ayres, "Fair Driving: Gender and Race Discrimination in Retail Car Negotiations" (1991) 104 *Harvard Law Review* 817–72; Ian Ayres, "Further Evidence of Discrimination in New Car Negotiations and Estimates of Its Cause" (1995) 94 *Michigan Law Review* 109–47.
16. Lisa Rice & Erich Schwartz, Jr., "Discrimination When Buying a Car: How the Color of Your Skin Can Affect Your Car Shopping Experience," National Fair Housing Alliance, January 11, 2018, https://nationalfairhousing.org/resource/discrimination-when-buying-a-car-how-the-color-of-your-skin-can-affect-your-car-shopping-experience/.
17. Jonathan Lanning, "Evidence of Racial Discrimination in the $1.4 Trillion Auto Loan Market," ProfitWise News and Views, January 2023, www.chicagofed.org/publications/profitwise-news-and-views/2023/discrimination-auto-loan-market.
18. Peter Weber, "How Tesla's Direct Sales Model Is Roiling the Car Dealership Industry," June 21, 2023, The Week, https://theweek.com/us/1024416/tesla-vs-car-dealerships.
19. Cherise Threewit, "Car Brans with the Best Warranty Coverage in 2025," 2025, U.S. News & World Report, https://cars.usnews.com/cars-trucks/advice/which-automaker-has-the-best-warranty.
20. Transcript, "Auto Distribution: Current Issues and Future Trends," Workshop Hosted by the Federal Trade Commission, January 19, 2016, www.ftc.gov/system/files/documents/public_events/895193/auto_distribution_transcript.pdf; David Sappington, "Is There Rationale for Warranty Reimbursement Laws," www.ftc.gov/system/files/documents/public_events/895193/panel_2_-_sappington.pdf.
21. *Tesla, Inc. v. Louisiana Automobile Dealers Association*, 677 F Supp 3d 417, 431 (E.D. La. 2023).
22. Peter Valdes-Dapena, "Tesla's Fight with America's Car Dealers," CNN, May 20, 2013, https://money.cnn.com/2013/05/20/autos/telsa-car-dealers.

23. Patrick George, "Used Fisker Karmas Are Selling For 50% Off MSRP," Jalopnik, May 17, 2013, http://jalopnik.com/used-fisker-karmas-are-selling-for-50-off-msrp-508187464.
24. Jonathan Collegio, "Should Tesla (and Other Auto Manufacturers) Be Able to Sell Cars Directly to Consumers?," Our Energy Policy, October 23, 2014, www.ourenergypolicy.org/should-tesla-and-other-auto-manufacturers-be-able-to-sell-cars-directly-to-consumers/#comments.
25. "Franchise System," National Automobile Dealers Association, www.nada.org/GetTheFacts (last visited February 15, 2025).
26. John O'Dell, "Why Tesla Should Stop Fighting Auto Dealers," CNN, March 18, 2014, www.cnn.com/2014/03/18/opinion/odell-tesla-new-jersey (opining that "car dealerships are important corporate citizens, pumping into the national economy hundreds of millions of sales-tax dollars, tens of millions of dollars in charitable contributions and billions of dollars in paychecks").
27. Bureau of Labor Statistics, Employment, Hours, and Earnings from the Current Employment Statistics Survey (National), https://data.bls.gov/timeseries/CES4244110001?amp%253bdata_tool=XGtable&output_view=data&include_graphs=true.
28. Bureau of Labor Statistics, Average hourly earnings of production and nonsupervisory employees, automobile dealers, not seasonally adjusted, https://data.bls.gov/timeseries/CEU4244110008?amp%253bdata_tool=XGtable&output_view=data&include_graphs=true.
29. Bureau of Labor Statistics, CPI Inflation Calculator, https://data.bls.gov/cgi-bin/cpicalc.pl?cost1=19.71&year1=201401&year2=202401.
30. Ally Financial, "Auto Dealers Increase Charitable Giving, Focus on Local Communities," PR Newswire, October 13, 2014, https://media.ally.com/2014-10-13-Auto-dealers-increase-charitable-giving-focus-on-local-communities.

5   LEGACIES IN THE CROSSFIRE

Mary Barra became CEO of General Motors (GM) on January 15, 2014, just when her counterpart at Tesla, Elon Musk, was turning up the heat on Detroit. Barra, the granddaughter of Finnish immigrants, was a historic hire for GM and the car industry more generally. She was not only the first woman to run one of Detroit's Big Three automakers or any major car company, but she was also a GM "lifer" *par excellence*. Barra began working at GM as an eighteen-year-old, using her pay from inspecting fender panels and hoods to finance her college education at what was then known as General Motors Institute (now Kettering University). She showed great potential while working a variety of engineering and administrative jobs at GM, and the company paid for her to get an MBA at Stanford's business school. From there, Barra continued her meteoric rise through the company ranks, working a number of top positions in engineering, manufacturing, and supply chain before landing the CEO position.

Mary Barra is the poster child for the American corporate dream of "the janitor can rise to CEO with hard work and perseverance." Millions of people watched her story with admiration and hope. Maybe there was hope for women in the corporate world. Maybe there was hope for the children of immigrants who started on the ground floor. Maybe there was hope for the Detroit auto industry. Maybe there was even hope for Detroit itself.

Living just a few miles from Detroit, I watched Barra's rise with mixed feelings. On the one hand, everyone loves a feel-good story, and Barra's story certainly seems to be that. On the other hand, it's sometimes hard to feel optimistic about Detroit's future. Like everyone who lives in southeastern Michigan, I have long rooted for the Motor City's return to greatness. Once a bustling metropolis of over two million people and the nation's fourth-largest city, Detroit is now a shell of its former glory with a population barely a quarter of its 1950 peak. Like many of its famous car businesses, the city has survived bankruptcy and struggled to get back on its feet. The city's past, present, and future seem tied to the car industry. Could Mary Barra really pull it off?

A low point arrived on January 8, 2020, six years into Barra's tenure as GM CEO. One important predictor of the future is stock prices. A company's stock price represents the net present value of the company's predicted future income streams. On January 8, 2020, Tesla's market capitalization exceeded the *combined* market capitalization of GM and Ford. Even though Tesla had only a small fraction of GM and Ford's sales, Wall Street was predicting that, in the near future, Silicon Valley would run roughshod over Detroit. Elon Musk was going to bury Mary Barra.

You have to feel for Mary Barra and the Big Three. After a near-death experience during the Financial Crisis of 2008–2009, they emerged as leaner and meaner fighting machines, eager to show America and the world that they were back in the business of building cars that Americans wanted to buy. Then, just a few years later, along came Elon Musk with a brand-new, sexy American car company marketing electric vehicle (EV) technology in which Detroit had never significantly invested and was very far behind. When Consumer Reports labeled the Model S the best-performing car they have ever tested, that had to sting in the city across the river from Windsor. Not only that, but Tesla had none of the legacies' baggage like onerous union contracts, stuffy management culture, or dinosaur brands. Or its expensive and nearly impossible to shed franchised dealer networks.

The latter point was a particularly sore one for Detroit. The legacy car companies had long had a "frenemy" relationship with their dealer networks, relying on their partnership to sell and market their brands, but chafing at the dealers' incessant deployment of legal and political processes to prevent dealer terminations, requiring the manufacturers to pay them exorbitant fees for service, and otherwise limiting the manufacturers' flexibility to manage distribution. Now, Musk was announcing that Tesla would bypass the dealers altogether.

A new entrant that already had a huge technological and business advantage was announcing that it wouldn't play by the established rules of the game.

Mary Barra and the legacies had three choices. First, they could side with their dealers and fight Tesla's direct sales model legally and politically. Second, they could stay out of the dealer wars with Tesla and just focus on developing EVs to catch up with Tesla. Third, they could jump on the direct sales bandwagon, agree with Tesla that flexibility to sell directly was important to selling EVs, and argue that if Tesla should be allowed to sell direct, so should they.

Many executives inside the legacies favored the third option. I know this for a fact because some of them have called me, asked for anonymity and confidentiality, and informed me that many insiders were fighting internally for their companies to go for option 3. But option 3 was nuclear. The dealers were already raging over Tesla's direct sales strategy. If the legacies had tried the same strategy – not only cutting them out of new business but reducing or eliminating their existing business – the dealers would have gone apoplectic.

Further, whereas Tesla had a creditable textual argument in many states that the direct sales prohibitions did not apply to a manufacturer that didn't use dealers at all, and an unassailable argument that a pure direct sales model was not in the contemplation of the legislatures that passed the relevant statutes, the legacies could not make those arguments. Detroit competing against its own dealers was exactly what the legislatures had prohibited. To be sure, the legacies would have had strong arguments that circumstances had changed since the mid twentieth century – that the manufacturer market was far more competitive, that the dealers were no longer mom-and-pops, that the dealers no longer needed legal protections against direct sales, and that, if they did, those protections could be less onerous than total bans on direct sales. But there was no question that advancing those arguments would risk Armageddon with the dealers.

Most legacy manufacturers chose option 2 – staying out of the Tesla wars. To my knowledge, none of the foreign manufacturers – Asian or European – took a position. This was not because they didn't have a dog in the fight. Tesla's flashy entry and direct sales model were consequential to Toyota and Volkswagen (VW), as they were to GM and Ford. But the foreign manufacturers appear to have concluded, probably wisely, that Tesla's wars were a no-win situation for them and decided to keep their powder dry.

So too did Chrysler (Stellantis Group, today). Perhaps Chrysler decided to stay out of the Tesla wars because, with its near-death experience during the Financial Crisis and Fiat's acquisition of the company in 2014, Chrysler wasn't looking to make itself anyone's political target. Like other automakers, Chrysler may also have been taking the long view and realizing that, eventually, it too would need flexibility in how to sell EVs. In 2022, there were media reports that Stellantis was quietly looking for ways to follow in Tesla's footsteps and sell EVs direct to consumers.[1] (Stellantis CEO called its direct sales strategy a win for consumers, a win for manufacturers, and a win for dealers. The dealers are reportedly skeptical about how a sales strategy that bypasses them counts as a win.)

On the other hand, Ford, and especially GM, chose option 1 – backing their dealers in opposing Tesla's right to sell direct. For example, in the Michigan battles discussed in more detail in Chapter 6, Ford and GM successfully exerted their political might to support the dealers' efforts to block Tesla.[2] While I am not privy to everything that happened behind the scenes in the back halls of state legislatures, governors' mansions, and state motor vehicle commissions, there is a public record of GM (much more than Ford) taking a leading role in opposing Tesla's right to sell direct, especially in rust belt states such as Michigan, Ohio, and Indiana, where GM has a major presence. For example, in Indiana, GM publicly supported the dealer lobby's unsuccessful effort to amend Indiana law to prohibit direct sales even by companies that do not employ franchised dealers. "Whether a company creates an electric car, a gas-powered car or one run by solar energy, the same basic rules should be applied across the board," Jason Wetzel, GM's regional manager for public policy, testified at a legislative hearing in 2016.[3] GM stuck with the same "everyone should play by the same rules" messaging in response to an inquiry from the Wall Street Journal about why it was playing an increasingly aggressive role in the dealers' fight against Tesla. A GM spokesman said that "GM believes that all industry participants should operate under the same rules and requirements on fundamental issues that govern how we sell, service and market our products."[4] After losing the fight to block Tesla in Indiana, GM vowed to continue the fight against direct sales in the rest of the country.[5]

The story in Ohio is particularly interesting because of how candidly GM spelled out its arguments against Tesla. In 2014, Tesla obtained a license from the Bureau of Motor Vehicles to open stores in Cincinnati and Columbus. The car dealers reacted as usual, claiming that Ohio's longstanding licensing rules had "been thrown upside down."[6] But then, in a rare moment of compromise, the dealers and Tesla struck a bargain. Tesla would be allowed to open up to three stores in Ohio, but the legislation would be gerrymandered effectively to apply only to Tesla. Legislation to this effect passed in the legislature and headed to the desk of the Republican governor (and later Donald Trump nemesis) John Kasich.

GM was understandingly unhappy. It was one thing for Tesla to squeeze through existing loopholes, but legislation appearing to give Tesla special privileges was a bridge too far. GM wrote a letter to Governor Kasich, urging him to veto the legislation.[7] It began by stressing its economic contributions to the state of Ohio and then asserted its opposition to "unique, favorable protection" for Tesla. What came next was particularly interesting. GM pointed out the "highly competitive" nature of the car market and asserted that "Tesla would gain a distinct competitive advantage by avoiding restrictions that all other auto manufacturers face in Ohio."

Step back for a minute and consider the implications of GM's argument. In earlier chapters, we saw that there is an inherent contradiction in the dealers' arguments against direct sales. On the one hand, they claim that it is unworkable as a business matter and doomed to fail. On the other hand, they claim that it is *too good* a business model and undermines their competitive position. GM offered no equivocation on this point. Direct sales represents "a distinct competitive advantage." Allowing Tesla to do it but not GM would place GM at an unfair competitive disadvantage.

But then why advocate for GM to be able to do it too? If direct sales represent a competitive advantage, that must be because direct sales are more efficient or cost less than franchised dealer sales. As a matter of public policy, if there's an uneven competitive playing field because one competitor can do something efficient that the other is blocked from doing, the right answer is to remove the block from the second competitor, not place it on the first. But GM was arguing just the opposite: that an inefficient regulation should be imposed on Tesla so that GM could compete.

Indeed, GM's political muscling against Tesla may be even worse than arguing for a regulatory lowest common denominator. In 1986, law professors Tom Krattenmaker and Steve Salop published what became a classic law review article showing how companies can exclude or marginalize competitors through "raising rivals' costs."[8] Here's how that might work. Suppose two competitors use the same, environmentally sensitive energy source, but one uses it for 15 percent of its energy needs while the second uses it for half its energy needs. Ordinarily, a company does not want to see its costs go up, but if the costs of this energy source increase, the first company will obtain a significant competitive advantage over its competitor. So the first company lobbies for environmental regulations that will dramatically increase the costs of this energy source. Even though its costs will increase, the company will more than make it up through increased market share and profits.

GM's political strategy toward direct sales looks like a similar raising rivals' costs tactic. In Chapter 2, we saw that many of the reasons that Tesla and other EV manufacturers have chosen direct sales go to things that are unique to EVs – the novelty of the technology, the different service profile, and so on. While GM had tried to roll out an electric car – the EV1 – as far back as 1996, that rollout was a failure and GM stuck with internal combustion cars long into the twenty-first century. It did not roll out its first mass-market EV – the Chevy Bolt – until 2016. Even in 2024, EV sales amounted to less than 3 percent of GM's total volume.[9] GM was selling gas-powered cars in competition with Tesla's EVs. Contrary to GM's "level the playing field" arguments, making EV sales operate under the same rules as gas-powered cars would not put EVs and gas-powered cars on a level playing field. It would significantly disadvantage the sale of EVs and hence preserve GM as a market leader for internal combustion cars. *Raising rivals' costs.*

Raising rivals' costs strategies can backfire, and that's exactly what's happening with GM. It lost the battle in Ohio. Kasich signed the bill, and Tesla got its three stores. GM also lost the battle in Indiana and eventually in Michigan. But GM lost more than just the battle to block Tesla. It also lost the opportunity to advance the other side of the argument – that if Tesla and other EV start-ups could use a direct sales model, then so should GM (at least as to EVs).

GM has had plenty of opportunities to come in on the side of direct sales for all and has almost invariably spurned them. What happened in Colorado in 2020 is a good case in point. In 2010, in response to GM's bankruptcy, the Colorado legislature passed a ban on direct sales that was intended to protect GM dealers from losing their franchises.[10] The Lamar Bus Company, which was headquartered in Denver (and had recently gone through a bankruptcy of its own) and sold directly to its corporate customers, protested that it should be exempt from the law. Apparently without any great controversy, the Colorado direct sales prohibition made an exception for any company that was in operation in 2009 and sold only directly to customers.

When Tesla came along a few years later, the company licked its chops. The loophole fit Tesla perfectly. The company had been in continuous existence since 2003, and it sold only direct. Tesla opened a store in Colorado. The dealers weren't happy about it, but the law was clearly on Tesla's side. As we saw in Chapter 3, it's a lot harder to pass a new law than to hunker down under an existing one.

Tesla was fine, but by 2019 a whole new crop of EV start-ups, led by Rivian, were in the same boat that Tesla had to row in many other states. Rivian saw Colorado as a ripe market for its outdoor adventure, environmentally conscious brand. The law inadvertently exempted Tesla, but that was hardly fair to other EV start-ups. Noting "substantial interest from Coloradans" in its products, Rivian led a coalition of other EV start-ups, environmental groups, and pro-consumer groups in lobbying for a legislative amendment allowing other EV companies to sell direct too. In 2019, a bill was introduced in the Colorado legislature that would allow all EV-only manufacturers to sell direct. Predictably, the Colorado Automobile Dealers Association ("CADA") opposed the bill, and the bill went nowhere.

In 2020, the Rivian-led coalition tweaked its strategy. The new bill it pushed would allow *any* manufacturer to sell EVs direct. GM, Ford, and other legacies would still have to sell their internal combustion cars through their franchised dealers, but they could compete on a level playing field with the EV start-ups by opening their own EV stores. Now the "everyone plays by the same rules" argument that GM had made in Ohio was off the table.

The EV coalition reached out to GM and invited it to join in supporting the Colorado legislation. GM was in a quandary. It could hardly take a public position against a bill that would give it flexibility to compete with Tesla and the other EV start-ups. On the other hand, if the dealers had been miffed about the 2019 bill, the 2020 version had the veins bulging on their foreheads. CADA's outside counsel issued a statement saying that the 2020 bill would "substantially undercut the significant investments that Colorado dealers make in their dealerships and their representation of their manufacturers in the market."[11] Not ready to take on its dealers but also apparently reconsidering its backfired strategy in Indiana, Ohio, and Michigan, GM stayed frozen on the sidelines. The dealers continued to oppose any direct sales bill, but had to content themselves with stripping the language allowing direct sales of any EV. The bill passed in essentially its 2019 form, allowing Rivian and other EV-only companies to sell direct, but holding the line as to the legacies. Once again, GM had missed an opportunity to advance the only viable version of its 2014 argument that there should be a level playing field for EV sales.

An exemption for direct sales that was limited to Tesla or EV-only manufacturers disadvantaged GM when the competition was internal combustion versus EV, but it started becoming existential as GM began to transition toward EVs as well. Although the pace of EV acceptance in the market has been uneven for a variety of reasons, the handwriting is on the wall for the internal combustion engine. In 2022, the California Air Resources Board established a rule requiring that 100 percent of new cars and light trucks sold in California be zero-emission vehicles by 2035.[12] The Biden Administration's Environmental Protection Agency promulgated a new emissions rule for light-duty and medium-duty vehicles that would require up to two-thirds of new cars and light trucks sold in the United States to be EVs within eight years. While the Trump Administration may roll back those requirements, there is little doubt that a massive transition toward EVs has begun.

GM had a year's jump on California, announcing in 2021 that it would produce only EVs by 2035.[13] But how will it sell those EVs? For the reasons we examined in Chapter 2, almost every EV start-up has reached the conclusion that selling through franchised dealers isn't viable. As it's tried to transition toward EV sales, GM has learned the hard way that getting its dealers excited about selling EVs isn't easy. In 2020, GM told its 880 Cadillac dealers that they would need to invest about $200,000 in upgrades in EV chargers, tooling, and training to begin selling EVs.[14] Many of the dealers balked and demanded that GM buy them out instead. In the end, 150 dealers opted for buyouts, costing GM between $300,000 and $1 million each.

Mary Barra finally seems to have come to the realization that a direct sales approach is critical to GM's ability to compete in the EV market. In 2022, Barra was asked point-blank whether GM would consider switching to a direct-to-consumer model.[15] She responded with the obligatory statement that "over the long term, our dealers are a strategic asset. They have the relationship in the community with the customers." But she then quickly pivoted to the disclaimer that "our offering is going to be, what does the customer want?" If customers wanted to literally "kick the tires" at a dealer, they would have that choice, but if they wanted to buy online like they could choose to do with Tesla and other EV start-ups, that option would be available to them too. In the same year as Barra made these comments, GM announced that it would launch a Tesla-style direct sales approach in China.[16] In 2023, it began selling the Cadillac Lyriq on a direct-to-consumer basis in Switzerland, with a rollout of the same model in France and Sweden in 2024.[17] In the United States, however, GM remains largely stuck in a regulatory cul-de-sac that it bears responsibility for shaping. Not just in Colorado, but in other important states like Florida,[18] recent direct sales legislation has allowed EV-only companies to sell direct, but denied that same opportunity to the legacies. GM now finds itself in the worst possible position, where EV mandates are coming, and the start-ups can sell direct but GM can't. If GM was right in 2014 that direct sales represents a significant competitive advantage, is it any wonder that Tesla's stock price exceeds GM and Ford's?

For its part, Ford's alliance with GM in opposing direct sales was short-lived. In 2019, the company invested half a billion dollars in

Rivian, which at a minimum would have made it awkward for Ford to continue to take the dealers' side in the direct sales wars. The company rolled out a direct-to-consumer sales model in China, which was not a success.[19] Nonetheless, in 2023 the company announced a plan to "leapfrog" dealers in the sale of EVs in the United States.[20] Ford CEO Jim Farley described the company's new strategy in terms that sound suspiciously like those proposed by Elon Musk a decade earlier: "Model E customers will have flexible purchase options, online, in the store, with transparent pricing that they don't have to haggle over, and remote vehicle delivery, and later pick up as well."[21] Also like Tesla, Ford announced that it intends "to curtail vehicle inventory and pivot away from TV advertising." Ford's new model may not be quite as radical as it sounds, as two-thirds of Ford's existing dealerships would partner with Ford in some way to implement the plan. Some dealers seem to have accepted that a revised model in which the manufacturer takes on most of the significant sales decisions but the dealer isn't cut out entirely is better for their interests than the Tesla model. As we'll see in Chapter 10, however, other dealers are fighting even these modest shifts in Ford's distribution strategy. In any event, Ford clearly learned that the one-size-fits-all distribution model of the 1950s was not viable as to the new generation of cars and buyers.

Meanwhile, other legacy car companies are cautiously searching for a way out. Speaking on an earnings call in 2023, Volvo CEO Jim Rowan rattled Volvo's US dealers by announcing that Volvo would pursue a direct sales strategy.[22] "It seems strange for me coming from the consumer electronics and technology industry that you can sell a product which is $40, $50, $60,000 of value to a customer that you never speak to pre-sales and you never speak to post-sales," he said. A spokesperson for Volvo's Retail Advisory Board objected that "[w]e do not feel respected or valued as partners with his comments."[23] Perhaps not, but the dealers still have the upper hand against direct sales by the legacies, including those like Volvo that had nothing to do with the origins of the dealer franchise laws or their perpetuation during the Tesla wars.

Honda and VW are facing even more pronounced threats from the car dealers as they dip their toes into the water of new partnerships or business strategies that could allow them to innovate in the way they build and sell cars. Honda has announced a partnership with Sony to roll out an EV called the Afeela by 2026. Early reviews have been glowing. One car industry analyst says that

> Sony Honda Mobility grabbed a cup of Porsche 911 and an ounce of Lucid Air put them in a shaker with ice and served up this delightful sedan. In an age where almost every car has enough styling for three or four cars, the Afeela is a minimalist sight for sore eyes, with gorgeous cab-rearward proportions and a fabulously low roofline. From the clamshell hood to the heckblende tail lights, this is just a clean piece of design.[24]

Meanwhile, VW is bringing its Cupra EV, described as "Europe's hottest brand," stateside.[25] VW also is reviving the Scout brand (an early SUV built by International Harvester from the 1960s to 1980s) as an EV and plans to sell the South Carolina-built Scout pickup trucks and SUVs directly to consumers.

While the American public might be pumped at the prospect of getting their hands on these cars, the dealers seem to be deflated, or, more accurately, gearing up for a fight. Although neither Honda nor VW has announced that they will try to sell direct, their temerity in remaining silent on how they plan to sell has the dealers in a tizzy. NADA Chairman Geoffrey Pohanka told Automotive News: "Silence speaks. The fact that they haven't announced that they will go through dealers indicates they may not."[26] Pohanka threatened NADA-backed lawsuits against Honda and VW if they dared to circumvent the dealers and go direct. Meanwhile, the Automotive Trade Association Executive group took out an ad in Automotive News making the threat explicit.[27] Asserting that "America's franchised dealers are excited to sell and service the Scout and Afeela brands," the dealers reminded Honda and VW that "companies directly or indirectly affiliated with an established original equipment manufacturer are prohibited by state law from selling new motor vehicles without the use of franchised dealers across most of the country. To avoid potential legal challenges across the nation and ensure full compliance with applicable laws and regulations, the surest path to sales success is through franchised dealers."[28] The most charitable thing that can be said about this letter is that an advertisement in the trade press beats a horse's head in the bed.

As much as they fought Tesla, the dealers are sending out a "you ain't seen nothing yet" message as to any defection by the legacies. The first decade of EVs was defined by wars between the start-ups and dealers; the second decade may be defined by wars between the dealers and the legacies. The legacies did themselves no favors by the way they navigated the Tesla dealer wars, either staying on the sidelines or actively supporting the dealers. The window to take a principled stand in favor of flexibility in distribution strategies was open, and they failed to take advantage.

While many legacies appear to be thinking hard about direct sales, they are far from uniform in signaling a desire to shift toward some direct sales of their own. In 2022, Bob Carter, Toyota North America's long-time executive vice president of sales, was asked about his view on direct sales during a NADA forum in New York.[29] Mr. Carter responded that if someone were to give him "one reason why you think direct sales is the direction of the future, and I'll give you 20 reasons why I think it's a disaster waiting to happen."[30] I wasn't at the NADA forum (I don't know if they would have let me in), but I imagine that thunderous applause must have broken out in the auditorium. Carter went on to guarantee the dealers that Toyota sees them as a competitive advantage and has no intention of abandoning them. At a minimum, this is impeccable political theater if you're in NADA country. It may also be sincere, and it may be true for now and change down the road. Different companies will try different strategies to sell EVs, and experimentation and competition will determine which ones work the best. That is to say, experimentation and competition *should* determine the winners and losers, assuming that the law does not straightjacket the legacies' choices. If it does, the injury will be at least partially self-inflicted.

As this book is written, Mary Barra and the legacies may still have a chance to pitch their way out of the legal and regulatory bind that they have gotten themselves into. For legal, political, and business reasons, that strategy may not involve a complete adoption of the Tesla direct sale model. To repeat a point made throughout this book, there is no general reason to think that the Tesla model is the best one for everyone everywhere always. Nor is the opposite true – the rigid franchise dealer model of the 1950s isn't the best for everyone everywhere always either. Distribution strategies need to adapt to changing technological, business, and social conditions. And, as we'll see in Chapter 6, they must account for changing political conditions too.

Notes

1. Breana Noble, "Stellantis Says Direct Sales Model Could Be a 'win-win-win.' Dealers Aren't Sure," The Detroit News, April 5, 2022, www.detroitnews.com/story/business/autos/chrysler/2022/04/05/stellantis-tesla-direct-sales-model-dealers/7067748001/.
2. Justin Lloyd-Miller, "Tesla's Public Appeal Falls Short as Michigan Bans Direct Sales," Cheat Sheet: Autos, October 22, 2014, https://web.archive.org/web/20170428120953/ www.cheatsheet.com/automobiles/teslas-public-appeal-falls-short-as-michigan-bans-direct-sales.html/ ("We applaud Gov. Snyder's action of signing HB 5606. The bill will provide a level playing field for all automobile manufacturers selling vehicles in Michigan...." (quoting Ford)); Jared Meyer, "'Anti-Tesla Bill' Means Economic Loss for Michigan," Manhattan Institute, October 26, 2014, https://manhattan.institute/article/anti-tesla-bill-means-economic-loss-for-michigan-2 (reporting that both GM and Ford supported the Michigan bill); David Shepardson, "GM Backs Anti-Tesla Michigan Bill," The Detroit News, October 21, 2014, www.detroitnews.com/story/business/autos/general-motors/2014/10/21/tesla-bill-michigan/17662581 ("We believe that House Bill 5606 will help ensure that all automotive manufacturers follow the same rules to operate in the State of Michigan; therefore, we encourage Governor Snyder to sign it...." (quoting GM)).
3. Ibid.
4. Mike Ramsey & Gautham Nagesh, "Tesla Fights GM-Backed Effort to Halt Direct-to-Consumer Sales," The Wall Street Journal, February 24, 2016, www.wsj.com/articles/tesla-fights-gm-backed-effort-to-halt-direct-to-consumer-sales-in-indiana-1456375012.
5. Dana Hull, "Tesla Blocks GM's Challenge to Direct Sales in Indiana," Automotive News, February 25, 2014, www.autonews.com/article/20160225/RETAIL07/302259966/tesla-blocks-gm-s-challenge-to-direct-sales-in-indiana.
6. Julie Carr Smyth, "Ohio Auto Dealers Fight Tesla over Sales Model," Associated Press, March 17, 2014, https://apnews.com/article/technology-ohio-john-kasich-climate-and-environment-3bd1ae7919bb4be7a02756cdfcb91632.
7. Letter from Selim Bingol, Senior Vice President, Global Communications & Public Policy, General Motors, to John Kasich, Governor of Ohio, March 5, 2014.
8. Thomas G. Krattenmaker & Steven C. Salop, "Anticompetitive Exclusion: Raising Rivals' Costs to Achieve Power Over Price" (1986) 96 *The Yale Law Journal* 209–93.

9. Mark Kane, "GM's U.S. EV Sales Decreased 21% In Q1 2024 As Bolt EVs Fade," InsideEVs, April 2, 2024, https://insideevs.com/news/714708/gm-us-ev-sales-2024q1/.
10. Tamara Chuang, "Electric-Vehicle Makers Want to Sell Directly to Coloradans, Dealers Say That's a 'Solution in Search of a Problem.'" The Colorado Sun, February 17, 2020, https://coloradosun.com/2020/02/17/electric-vehicle-makers-direct-sales-colorado-bill/.
11. Ibid.
12. "California Moves to Accelerate to 100% New Zero-Emission Vehicle Sales by 2035," California Air Resources Board, August 25, 2022, https://ww2.arb.ca.gov/news/california-moves-accelerate-100-new-zero-emission-vehicle-sales-2035.
13. Steven Mufson, "General Motors to Eliminate Gasoline and Diesel Light-Duty Cars and SUVs by 2035," The Washington Post, January 28, 2021, www.washingtonpost.com/climate-environment/2021/01/28/general-motors-electric/.
14. Michael Wayland, "About 150 Cadillac Dealers Take GM Buyouts Rather than Invest in EVs," CNBC, December 4, 2020, www.cnbc.com/2020/12/04/about-150-cadillac-dealers-take-gm-buyouts-rather-than-invest-in-evs.html.
15. "Influencers with Andy Serwer: Mary Barra," yahoo! finance, May 5, 2022, https://finance.yahoo.com/video/influencers-andy-serwer-mary-barra-110000090.html.
16. Eva Fox, "GM to Launch Tesla-Style Direct Sales Model in China, Ford to Pressure Dealers to Cut Delivery Costs to Compete with Tesla," Tesmanian, September 10, 2022, www.tesmanian.com/blogs/tesmanian-blog/gm-to-launch-a-tesla-style-direct-sales-model-in-china-ford-to-pressure-dealers-to-cut-delivery-costs-to-compete-with-tesla#google_vignette.
17. Jamie L. LaReau, "GM Announces Start of EV Sales in France as it Slowly Reenters Europe," Detroit Free Press, February 26, 2024, www.freep.com/story/money/cars/general-motors/2024/02/26/gm-electric-vehicles-france-europe/72743365007/.
18. Caden DeLisa, "DeSantis Hits the Brakes on Direct-to-Consumer Auto Sales," The Capitolist, June 9, 2023, https://thecapitolist.com/desantis-hits-the-brakes-on-direct-to-consumer-auto-sales/.
19. Brad Anderson, "Ford Axes Direct EV Sales in China Following Weak Demand for Mustang Mach-E," Carscoops, September 27, 2023, www.carscoops.com/2023/09/ford-axes-direct-sales-in-china-following-weak-demand-for-its-evs/.
20. "Ford Charts a New Path: Plans to Sidestep Dealerships through Online Car Sales," Energy Trend, June 12, 2023, www.energytrend.com/news/20230612-32290.html.
21. Ibid.

22. Chris Teague, "Volvo's CEO Rattles Dealer Network with Statements on Direct Sales," The Truth About Cars, February 12, 2023, www.thetruthaboutcars.com/cars/news-blog/volvo-s-ceo-rattles-dealer-network-with-statements-on-direct-sales-44499295.
23. Ibid.
24. Thomas Hundal, "Sony Honda Mobility's Afeela Prototype Is a Delightfully Minimalist Posh Electric Sedan," The Autopian, January 5, 2023, www.theautopian.com/sony-honda-mobility-afeela-prototype/.
25. Matt Hardigree, "America Is About to Get Europe's Coolest Car Brand and I'm Pumped," The Autopian, March 22, 2024, www.theautopian.com/america-is-about-to-get-europes-coolest-car-brand-and-im-pumped/.
26. Matt Hardigree, "Here's Why Dealers Are Sending Threats to Honda and Volkswagen," The Autopian, April 22, 2024, www.theautopian.com/heres-why-dealers-are-sending-threats-to-honda-and-volkswagen/.
27. Ibid.
28. Ibid.
29. Cliff Banks, "Direct-to-Consumer Model 'A Disaster Waiting to Happen' for Automakers," The Banks Report, April 17, 2022, https://thebanksreport.com/manufacturers/direct-to-consumer-model-a-disaster-waiting-to-happen-for-automakers/.
30. Ibid.

6 CRONY CAPITALISM IN THE MOTOR CITY

It was two weeks before the election, and Rick Snyder knew he had a big problem on his hands. The incumbent Republican governor of Michigan, Snyder, was locked in a close reelection campaign against former US Representative Mark Schauer, the Democratic nominee. Snyder was weighed down by negative approval ratings and political analysts considered the race a toss-up. And then the Tesla bill landed on his desk.

The timing couldn't have been worse for Snyder. On the one hand, Snyder had every reason to understand the importance of allowing companies to choose how to sell their products and consumers to choose how to buy them. He well understood distribution strategies in general and direct sales in particular. From 2005 to 2007, he had served as Chairman of the Board of Gateway Computers, which at the time sold its computers directly to consumers.[1] Moreover, Snyder understood the legal and policy questions well and had a disposition toward free market solutions. A graduate of the University of Michigan Law School (my employer) who is often described as "nerdy" and a "policy wonk," Snyder was ideologically aligned with the Mackinac Center, an influential Michigan-based libertarian think tank that has strongly backed Tesla in the direct sales wars. So Tesla had some hope that Snyder would veto the anti-Tesla bill.

On the other hand, the prevailing political winds made exercising the veto pen a highly risky strategy. The bill was backed by two powerful Republican constituencies – the car dealers' lobby and two of Detroit's Big Three – General Motors (GM) and Ford. Snyder didn't need his political consultants to tell him that antagonizing crucial supporters on the eve of the election wasn't a good idea. It was a moment of principle against politics. Which would prevail?

The story of the Tesla wars in Michigan deserves its own chapter. I may be biased in saying this, because they occurred in my backyard and I was on the front lines of many of the battles. But there's a good argument that the Michigan story has the most compelling ingredients of any state. Politically, the Wolverine State is as purple as they come (at least in state-wide elections), with control of the governor's mansion, attorney general's office, and legislature always up for grabs – as they were when Governor Snyder made his fateful choice in 2014. It is the home of a politically active car dealers' lobby, the Big Three, and another of the Big Three's frenemies – the United Auto Workers union – all of whom have different interests when it comes to car distribution. It also happens to be one of the homes of one of the electric vehicle (EV) start-ups – Rivian. Michigan is a microcosm of the Tesla wars across the country. The story of Tesla's fight to sell in Michigan spans a decade. There is political treachery, politician double-speak, shifting alliances worthy of *The Game of Thrones*, and – wait for it – fights over English grammar and usage.

The story starts in 1977, when Michigan came late to the party in banning direct sales. As noted in Chapter 1, the legislative history of the Michigan statute reveals that the statute was designed to address "the unequal power balance between dealers and manufacturers [that] leaves a great potential for arbitrary and unilateral decisions by manufacturers about contract arrangements"[2] by forbidding manufacturers "to compete with franchised dealers by offering the same services."[3] Here's how the legislature wrote the direct sales prohibition: "A manufacturer shall not ... [s]ell any new motor vehicle directly to a retail customer other than through its franchised dealers."

Anyone who has ever drafted a statute will tell you that it's a lot harder to get a law to say what you want than most people think. What exactly did the legislature mean that a manufacturer could not sell cars except through "its" franchised dealers? The wording of the statute just assumed that a manufacturer *had* franchised dealers. Did it mean that every manufacturer *must have* franchised dealers in order to sell? Or, did it mean that *if a manufacturer had franchised dealers*, it couldn't sell direct? At a minimum, the language of the statute was ambiguous. When statutes are ambiguous, courts typically interpret them by studying the bill's legislative history, including such things as legislative purpose – what the legislature was trying to accomplish. Such an inquiry would likely have led to the conclusion that, in 1977, the legislature wanted to protect franchised dealers from competition by their franchising manufacturers, not to prohibit car companies that didn't use franchised dealers from selling direct.

That's certainly a plausible reading of the statute, because it was what the car dealers' lobby feared the courts would do when the inevitable legal challenge to Tesla's direct sales strategy in Michigan arose. In 2014, the car dealers were gearing up to fight Tesla in Michigan when catastrophe struck. On September 15, the Massachusetts Supreme Judicial Court handed down its ruling discussed in Chapter 3, finding that Massachusetts' direct sales prohibition was intended to limit manufacturers from competing against their own dealers, not interbrand competition. The Michigan direct sales provision was worded somewhat differently but, like the Massachusetts provision, was in a dealers' bill of rights provision and had similar legislative history. The dealers worried that the Michigan courts would follow Massachusetts and find that the direct sales provision didn't apply to Tesla.

But the dealers hoped to avoid a big public fight in Michigan. It was still early days in the Tesla wars, and it wasn't clear which way the political winds were blowing. The dealers looked for a stealth path to shut down the apparent loophole in the Michigan statute. They found it two weeks after the Massachusetts decision. On October 1, 2014, an automotive dealer franchise bill that had been pending since May 2014 came to the floor of the Michigan senate.[4] The bill provided for an amendment to the auto franchise statute, but it only addressed titling fees and had nothing to do with direct distribution. The dealers and manufacturers had already worked out a compromise on titling fees, and the bill was ready to pass without controversy. When the bill came to the floor, Republican Senator John Hune, who reportedly received campaign contributions from the auto dealers and whose wife worked for a lobbying group that represented the auto dealers, introduced a floor amendment making a few seemingly modest "clean-up" changes to the bill.[5] One was to strike the word "its" from the portion of the statute prohibiting direct sales. Suddenly, instead of saying that a manufacturer had to distribute only through "its" franchised dealers, the statute said that a manufacturer had to distribute through franchised dealers. No longer could Tesla argue that the existing law applied only to manufacturers with franchise relationships. The grammar wars had begun.

The amended bill passed both houses of the legislature with a single dissenting vote. (The dissenting legislator objected on a different ground than direct sales.) Very few of the legislators had any idea that they were voting to block direct sales by Tesla. There was some other linguistic clean-up language in other parts of the bill, so most legislators apparently assumed striking the "its" was an insignificant technical change. The chair of the Democratic caucus was quoted as saying that the Democratic members of the legislature had no idea the floor amendment was aimed at Tesla.[6] When I visited Lansing and met with legislators in the Capitol sometime later, legislators on both sides of the aisle who had voted for the bill told me they had no idea that it was about Tesla. One veteran Republican angrily told me that, when the floor amendments came up, he suspected that it might be about Tesla and directly asked the amendment's sponsor, who assured him that it was not.

The legislature had been hoodwinked. As soon as the striking of "its" snuck through the legislature and headed to the governor's desk, a lobbyist for the car dealers called the governor's chief of staff and explained things quite clearly: The dealers were worried that Michigan courts would follow Massachusetts in interpreting the direct sales prohibition not to apply to companies that did not have franchised dealers at all. The striking of "its" was necessary to close that door.

The dealers did not admit that publicly. Instead, they engaged in amazing logical jujitsu, on the one hand claiming that Tesla was already prohibited from selling direct under the existing law and that the striking of "its" changed nothing, and on the other hand claiming that the amendment was necessary to ensure that everyone played by the same rules. Here it is in the voice of Terry Burns, executive vice president of the Michigan Auto Dealers Association: "One of the things that was added to the bill was a section that states this law applies to all manufacturers. There's no creation of new rules. If a manufacturer wants to come in and sell cars in the state of Michigan, they should probably follow Michigan law."[7]

I've been a law professor for over twenty years. If any of my students made an argument that a law simultaneously changed nothing and that it was necessary to correct an imbalance, they probably wouldn't be graduating from law school. Of course, Tesla immediately saw through it. Todd Maron, Tesla's General Counsel, noted with unassailable logic that "[p]eople don't introduce bills unless they intend to change the law," and "[s]econdly, people don't sneak language in at the last minute unless they know it will be consequential."[8] Upon hearing of the bill, Tesla immediately launched a public blitz and worked with the governor's office to veto the bill.

Enter Rick Snyder. The governor couldn't have wished for this dilemma on the eve of a close election, but there it was. Vetoing unanimous bi-partisan legislation before the election would have been politically risky, especially given the political power of the car dealers' lobby. And then GM and Ford weighed in, publicly supporting the bill.[9] Snyder now faced the unenviable prospect of vetoing legislation supported by two of Michigan's iconic car companies in order to help a scrappy upstart from California.

In order to obtain cover, Snyder asked the Michigan Attorney General for an opinion as to whether the existing law already prohibited pure direct distribution. Without citing any legal authority resolving the issue or acknowledging that it was at minimum contestable, the Attorney General's chief legal counsel replied that it did. Snyder then signed the bill, explaining that it was not anti-Tesla after all since Tesla was already prohibited from direct distribution.[10] His letter explaining his endorsement of the legislation is what, in automobile lore, they call "a real duesy."

Snyder began by stating that "[i]t appears that there has been a fair amount of misunderstanding over one aspect of this legislation." What Snyder did not say was that, while there had been plenty of "misunderstanding" in the legislature, the car dealers' lobbyists had explained it all to the governor's office quite clearly. Belying Snyder's position, the senator who had sponsored the floor amendment striking "its" publicly admitted that his motivation was to stop

Tesla from taking advantage of "an end-around."[11] Nonetheless, Snyder went on:

> This bill does not, as some have claimed, prevent auto manufacturers from selling automobiles directly to consumers at retail in Michigan. That is because this is already prohibited under Michigan law. The current law states that a manufacturer shall not "[s]ell any new motor vehicle directly to a retail customer other than through its franchised dealers...." The current language states plainly that a manufacturer can only sell new vehicles to consumers through its own network of franchised dealers.

As noted earlier, it was hardly "plain" what the previous version of the statute meant. The dealers certainly didn't think so, which is why they wanted "its" stricken, as they had told the governor's chief of staff.

What came next took the cake. Snyder offered the following explanation for the deletion of "its": "This change would appear merely to allow manufacturers who do not have their own franchised dealers to sell through another manufacturer's network of franchised dealers." So, with a straight face, Snyder was arguing that the purpose of the legislation was to allow Ford to sell F-150s through GM dealers and GM to sell Cadillacs through Chrysler dealers. Suffice it to say that, beyond the ridiculousness of that possibility as a business matter, there was not a shred of evidence that *anyone* in the legislature had meant anything of the kind.

Snyder then fell back on the Attorney General's opinion: "The bill does not eliminate the ability of manufacturers to conduct direct sales, because they did not have that right before I signed HB 5606 into law. They could only sell through franchised dealers, and this will remain the case under the new law." This was pure sophistry. Although it was plausible that a court would have taken the view expressed by the Attorney General, it was at least as plausible that a court would take the contrary view, which was the whole reason that the dealers had struck "its." It was as if a runner kneecapped a competitor, won the race, and then claimed that he would have won anyway since he was faster.

Snyder's pretense that the bill wasn't anti-Tesla fooled exactly no one. The following day, headlines across the country announced what had plainly happened in Michigan. CBS News announced that "Governor Snyder Signs Michigan Tesla Ban," CNN that "Tesla Blocked from Selling in Michigan," Forbes that "Michigan to Tesla Motors: You're Not Welcome," Reuters that "Michigan Becomes Fifth U.S. State to Thwart Direct Tesla Car Sales," and Road and Track that "GM Supports Anti-Tesla Bill in Michigan, Snyder Signs Into Law."[12] I counted over 30 similar stories in national media outlets, most of which skipped right over Snyder's protestation that the bill wasn't anti-Tesla and went straight to the direct sales issue. My favorite was a scathing editorial in the Wall Street Journal, usually Snyder's bosom buddy.[13] Under the headline "Rick Snyder Drives off the Road: Michigan's Pro-Market Governor Embraces the Car Dealer Cartel," the Journal's editorial board chastised Snyder for "throwing his principles over the side" in order to get reelected. A few weeks later, the Information Technology and Innovation Foundation awarded Michigan one of its dreaded "Luddite awards."[14] It wasn't a good look for Governor Snyder or the Wolverine State.

In his letter explaining his signature of the bill, Snyder had thrown a sop to Tesla, suggesting that the direct sales issue should remain open for reconsideration. He wrote that a "healthy, open discussion can and should be had over whether the current business model in Michigan should be changed," that "this discussion should consider, first and foremost, what is best for Michigan consumers, for expanding economic activity, and for innovation in our state," and that we "should always be willing to reexamine our business and regulatory practices with an eye toward improving the customer experience for our citizens and doing things in a more efficient and less costly fashion." Snyder urged "the Legislature to engage in this discussion and to make it a top priority in its next session."

Let's give Governor Snyder the benefit of the doubt and assume that he meant this sincerely. The problem was that good intentions don't easily translate into law. As we saw in Chapter 3, there is a strong status quo bias in law – it's hard to change things. Within a little over a year from Snyder's re-election in 2014, the Flint water crisis was in full swing and political priorities had shifted. Although many legislators were sympathetic to Tesla's position, not many of them were motivated to take on the car dealers' lobby, GM, and Ford. In 2016, a newly elected Republican Representative named Aaron Miller who was strongly committed to free market values introduced legislation similar to the California law that would have allowed manufacturers to sell direct to consumers so long as they didn't open a showroom within close proximity to their franchised dealers. The bill went nowhere.

In the meanwhile, Tesla was effectively shut out of Michigan. Not only could it not open sales or service centers, but state officials began taking aggressive interpretations of the law that would kneecap Tesla from almost any marketing activity in the state. In 2014, the Michigan Office of Investigative Services Business Compliance and Regulation Division sent Tesla a letter demanding that it immediately discontinue test drives after the state "learned" Tesla was "advertising appointments to test drive vehicles through a Tesla Product Specialist in Detroit."[15] Tesla faced legal risk if it even opened a gallery to showcase its vehicles. In fact, there was concern that Tesla might be breaking Michigan law if it even showed up at the Detroit Auto Show.

Meanwhile, there were thousands of Tesla owners in Michigan who had bought their cars online or in another state, and they were growing increasingly unhappy. Tesla was shut out of not only selling cars in Michigan but also of opening a service center. It was one thing to make a trip to Ohio to buy a car and quite another to drive there on a regular basis for service. For many Michiganders, the closest Tesla service center was in Columbus, Ohio, which was not only a three-hour-plus drive but also the home of the Ohio State Buckeyes. Let's just leave it at that.

As Governor Snyder's promise of speedy reexamination of the direct sales ban faded and Tesla owners agitated for action, Tesla considered its options. During this time, I had a number of calls with lawyers for the company considering possible paths forward. (Again, for the record, I never worked for Tesla, but I frequently gave them free advice.) Legislative relief seemed a dead end, and the only available option seemed to be a lawsuit challenging the direct sales ban. But Michigan was trickier than other states where a lawsuit could have clarified that the direct sales ban did not apply to companies that didn't employ franchised dealers. The dealers had schemed to close that possibility in the 2014 amendment. That left a constitutional challenge to Michigan's direct sales ban as the only viable option.

Here, the Tesla story intersects with bigger questions in the history of American constitutional law. The brief version is this. In the late nineteenth and early twentieth centuries, the Supreme Court invalidated state statutes that regulated economic activities because they conflicted with the Court's laissez faire interpretation of the Constitution. In the mid twentieth century, under pressure from the New Deal challenge to the Court's conservatism and President Franklin Roosevelt's court-packing plan, the Court reversed itself and abandoned its "substantive due process" scrutiny of socioeconomic regulation. On many occasions, the Court upheld state laws that were nakedly protectionist of special interests, stating that it wouldn't inquire into the laws' soundness as a matter of public policy because that job was for the legislature, not the courts. The door seemed to be shut to the kind of constitutional arguments that Tesla would have needed to make against Michigan's direct sales ban.

In a field closely related to cars – gasoline – the Supreme Court had upheld a statute prohibiting direct sales in the 1970s.[16] Responding to gasoline shortages during the oil crisis in 1973 and evidence that oil companies were favoring their own company-owned stations in allocations, Maryland enacted a prohibition on oil producers or refiners operating their own retail service stations in the state. *Exxon*, which operated thirty-six stations in Maryland, challenged the law under the Commerce Clause of Article I, Section 8, and also as a violation of its due process rights. Writing for the Court, Justice Stevens acknowledged that there was "some doubt about the wisdom of the statute" and that it might "frustrate rather than further the State's desired goal of enhancing competition," but held that the courts should not "sit as a superlegislature to weigh the wisdom of legislation." In other words, the Supreme Court accepted that Maryland's direct sales ban might well be terrible policy, but, reflecting the post-New Deal attitude, the Court wasn't going to weigh in on the merits of the law. If there was to be a remedy, it would have to be at the polls.

There are certainly ways to distinguish the *Exxon* case from state bans on direct sales of cars. In its 2001 case in Texas, Ford argued that *Exxon* turned on the specific facts about the oil crisis of the 1970s. The court didn't buy it. As discussed in Chapter 3, Ford lost its constitutional challenges. The more obvious point as to the EV start-ups is that they don't use independent retailers at all, so the whole point of both the Maryland scheme in *Exxon* and of the direct sales prohibitions as to automobiles simply doesn't apply. But while there are things to say to distinguish the particulars of *Exxon*, the overall attitude of the courts during the second half of the twentieth century was decidedly against the kinds of constitutional arguments that Tesla would need to make to invalidate the direct sales bans.

But that door has opened a bit in recent decades. A few lower federal courts have again begun to experiment with a limited version of review of state laws that limit competition or favor special interests. A good case in point is a 2002 decision of the US Court of Appeals,[17] which has jurisdiction over Michigan. The Tennessee Funeral Directors and Embalmers Act prohibited the sale of caskets by anyone not licensed as a funeral director. A group of plaintiffs who operated independent casket stores persuaded the court that the sales restriction lacked a rational basis under the Fourteenth Amendment's equal protection clause because the statute was designed to protect "a discrete interest group from economic competition," and that "is not a legitimate governmental purpose." Tesla could possibly take advantage of this ruling, and also of cases interpreting the Constitution's "commerce clause" as prohibiting states from discriminating against companies from other states, to challenge Michigan's direct sales ban.

The strategy had its risks. While some lower courts had cautiously opened the door to these kinds of legal arguments, other lower courts had held the door firmly shut. What the Supreme Court would say was unclear. Further, could Tesla really establish as a matter of law that the legislature's sole purpose in passing the 2014 amendment was to favor the car dealers and/or the Big Three in competition with Tesla? Tesla worried that it might lose that argument. Thus far, the company had taken a conservative legal strategy across the country. It had not yet lost on direct sales in any courtroom and wanted to keep its winning streak alive.

For two years, Tesla equivocated on whether to sue the state of Michigan. Then, in September 2016, with no action forthcoming on Snyder's admonition that the legislature reexamine the direct sales ban, Tesla filed its constitutional challenge in federal court in Grand Rapids. The state moved to dismiss, but the judge held that Tesla had stated a viable claim, if it could prove its allegations. The case proceeded into discovery, where Tesla sought evidence of contacts between the car dealers' lobby and the state. Among other things, Tesla sought phone records and internal communications between Republican Representative Jason Sheppard, Senator Hune (who had sponsored the anti-Tesla amendments in the Senate), and the car dealers' lobbyists.[18] Sheppard and Hune tried to block Tesla from getting access to their communications, but Judge Carmody ruled that they were "fair game" and allowed Tesla access.[19] Slowly, the company began to gather hard evidence of what had happened behind the scenes.

As with any good story, what happened next involved an unpredictable twist. For several years, the case trundled along in pretrial discovery and motion practice. Then, in 2019, two new sheriffs came to town. Democrat Gretchen Whitmer became governor, and, more importantly for our story, Democrat Dana Nessel became the first Jewish person and LGBT-identifying individual to be elected Attorney General of Michigan. For her part, Whitmer was not eager to pick a fight with the car dealers, GM, and Ford. But Nessel had little choice. As Attorney General, she was handed the Tesla lawsuit, which was slated to go to trial in the summer of 2020. Nessel reviewed the file, assessed the state's position, and decided to settle with Tesla.

Nessel had a fine needle to thread. As the state's chief legal officer, she could hardly be expected to concede that the state had acted unconstitutionally. Instead, taking a page out of the dealers' playbook, she decided that it was time for some creative reinterpretation of the Michigan statute. The law prohibited a car manufacturer from "selling" in the state or from opening its own service centers. But what exactly did that mean? The act of "selling" meant transferring title to the vehicle. And, while Tesla could not open a service center itself, the act said nothing about a Tesla subsidiary doing so.

In January 2020, Nessel and Tesla entered into a settlement agreement that ended Tesla's lawsuit against the state.[20] The settlement stipulated an unexpected interpretation of Michigan law. While Tesla couldn't "sell" in Michigan, "selling" meant transferring legal title to the vehicle, "not conducting demonstration drives; discussing prices, service, financing, leasing, and trade-ins with potential customers; helping potential customers configure a vehicle; facilitating ordering and purchase of a vehicle for which legal title transfers out-of-state; and facilitating customer transaction paperwork for a sale for which legal title transfers out-of-state" or delivering a vehicle to the customer. In other words, Tesla could run as many stores as it pleased in Michigan, doing everything that a traditional car dealership does, except that when it came time to push a button to execute the exchange of money for the vehicle title, the titling had to happen outside of Michigan. Apart from a few extra steps in registering the vehicle in Michigan, the customer would hardly notice a difference. As to service, the Attorney General and Tesla stipulated that "no provision of Michigan law prohibits employees of Tesla from performing warranty, recall, service, or repair work at a facility owned or operated by the Tesla Service Subsidiary on vehicles owned or leased by Tesla customers."

It was a stunning reversal in the Tesla wars. Without a legislative act or judicial decision, Tesla could effectively do whatever it wanted in Michigan. Besides the car dealers, the major loser was the Michigan treasury, which, as discussed in Chapter 5, stood to lose millions of dollars in revenues from Michigan residents whose Tesla purchases were counted as happening in other states. But Tesla's Michigan owners were ecstatic. Tesla was coming to Michigan.

The dealers were no doubt immensely frustrated that Tesla had escaped their trap, but they didn't give up. The next episode in the Tesla wars was the most interesting and revealing one yet. In the fall of 2020, Republicans in the Michigan legislature were at war with Governor Whitmer on COVID lockdown policy, and the dealers bet that the Governor would not be in the mood for a fight with the Republicans over car sales. The dealers drafted a new statute amending the Michigan franchised dealer act to reverse the interpretation of the existing law that Nessel and Tesla had stipulated to a few months before.[21] Now all of the things that Nessel and Tesla had stipulated were *not* "sales" would be considered sales, and manufacturers were prohibited from owning service centers either "directly" or "indirectly," which would have closed the loophole allowing manufacturers to run service centers through subsidiaries. Effectively, the ban on direct sales would once again become comprehensive and absolute. But the dealers allowed for one exception – the new statute would not apply to any "manufacturer that entered into a joint stipulation and motion for entry of dismissal" in the Tesla litigation and has not sold a single new motor vehicle in the state through a franchised dealer. In other words, the bill made a special carve-out for Tesla to avoid restarting Tesla's constitutional challenge.

So if the bill caved to Tesla, who was it aimed against? By the COVID era, a whole new crop of EV start-ups led by Rivian and Lucid were coming to market with the same direct sales strategy as Tesla. Further, the dealers were especially concerned that the Tesla settlement's interpretation of Michigan law might not be limited to EV-only manufacturers. If it wasn't "selling" for Tesla to open a showroom, give test drives, take trade-ins, set prices, establish financing, and deliver cars, why would those activities be "selling" for GM? The dealers blanched at the prospect.

The bill was sent to the House Government Operations Committee on September 24, 2020. I attended the hearing and testified virtually, as did Rivian, and some environmental groups. The hearing was interesting. The committee consisted of three Republicans and two Democrats. The three Republicans were clearly in the dealer's pocket. One Republican Representative spoke at some length about how he had bought an EV from a dealer and didn't see what the problem was. One Democrat – a progressive – was clearly hostile to Elon Musk, an Internet billionaire who was ostensibly seeking special privileges. (More on this in Chapter 7.) The other Democrat had clearly studied the issue, listened to the environmentalist lobby, and didn't see the fairness of allowing Tesla special privileges while blocking other EV start-ups. She seemed smart, and she seemed to get exactly what was going on. The Committee ended up voting to approve the legislation and send it on to the full House with all three Republicans in favor, the Progressive Democrat abstaining, and the other Democrat opposed.

What was most interesting, however, was not the hearing itself but the positioning that happened outside the hearing. For once, Tesla stayed on the sidelines. After all, the bill didn't take away its right to do what it wanted in Michigan and, if anything, advantaged Tesla by codifying the 2020 settlement *and* denying Rivian and other emerging competitors the right to compete on equal footing with Tesla. To be clear, the bill wasn't Tesla's fault, but nor did Tesla have any incentive to waste political capital opposing the bill.

On the other hand, for the first time since the beginning of the Tesla wars in Michigan, GM and Ford decided to stand up to the dealers on direct sales. The bill was not only going to shut them out of any flexibility with respect to distribution, but it was also going to cement a special privilege for Tesla, forever. GM and Ford submitted formal statements opposing the bill. So did the United Auto Workers union ("UAW"). That also was an interesting turn. Until then, organized labor had stayed out of the direct sales controversy, seeing it as someone else's issue. But the UAW had no great love for Elon Musk, whose workforce isn't unionized, and when they got wind of a car dealer bill that would have granted Tesla a special privilege as against Detroit, they joined their frenemies in GM and Ford management and took a stand against the bill.

By the time the bill left the Committee, it had the opposition of the Detroit car manufacturers, EV start-ups (other than Tesla), labor, environmental groups, consumer groups, free market groups, and pointy-headed academics. Has such a coalition ever come together in American history? It is a testament to the power of the car dealer's lobby that, despite the extraordinary coalition arrayed against the bill, it still made it out of committee.

It made it out of committee, but was dead on arrival in the House. For one, the bill was plainly unconstitutional in granting Tesla a special carve-out. Article 4, Section 29, of the Michigan Constitution prohibits "special acts," legislation that grants a special privilege to a single company. But even if the legislators didn't care about the Michigan constitution, they did care about the formidable opposition to the bill. The Republicans cared about not screwing GM, and the Democrats cared about not screwing the UAW. The car dealers huddled – or maybe this was their plan all along – and proposed a slight tweak to the bill. Never mind the Tesla carve-out. The statute would apply to everyone, effectively ending any possibility of direct sales or service in the state by anyone.

Instantly, the main players switched their musical chairs. GM, Ford, and the UAW went to neutral on the bill, and Tesla threw itself back into opposition mode. I don't know if anyone was giving the dealers legal advice, but if so, it wasn't very good. The dealers had traded unconstitutionality under the Michigan constitution for the prospect of unconstitutionality under the federal constitution, as the federal court in Grand Rapids had made clear in setting Tesla's challenge for trial. But legal niceties and trial prospects weren't at the top of the dealers' agenda. Here was a chance to undo the Tesla settlement and delay Tesla's entry once again.

With the sudden change in political alliances, the revised bill passed the Michigan House with predominantly Republican support. Cooler heads prevailed in the Senate. The bill never came up for a vote, died at the end of the legislative session, and never again saw the light of day. At least for now. To paraphrase Monty Python, no one expects the Spanish Inquisition, and no one expects the car dealers' lobby to ever give up on trying to block direct sales.

This time, the power of incumbency had worked in the favor of Tesla, Rivian, Lucid, and the other EV start-ups. In 2014, the dealers were able to change the law only by sneaking the word "its" out of the statute. Once a Tesla-sympathetic Attorney General cleverly established an interpretation of the law that the dealers hadn't expected, the burden of changing the law through a forthright assault on direct sales became much greater. This time, the dealers didn't even get through the legislature, much less to the desk of Governor Whitmer, who may well have exercised the veto that Governor Snyder had not.

In early 2023, Tesla opened a store in my hometown of Ann Arbor. After working with Tesla on the direct sales issue for almost a decade, I felt a certain degree of pride and vindication. I was also curious to see how Nessel's settlement agreement worked in practice. I walked into the store, was greeted by a perky young salesman, and asked him if he could sell me a Model X. He responded with enthusiasm: "Of course, let's get started!" The dour law professor in me came out, and I tried to explain that the correct answer to my question was "no, I can't *sell* you a car." He seemed genuinely puzzled at my explanation, but good-naturedly went along with it and then turned back to the more serious business of selling me a car. (For the record, I didn't buy a Tesla. Like most other people in Ann Arbor, I still drive an older Subaru that I bought from a dealer. Call me cheap.) Ah, the power of words. The dealers had played a tricky game with words in 2014, and it had come back to bite them.

From its racial, religious, social, economic, and political demographics to its conflicted attitudes toward direct sales, Michigan is a microcosm of America. With the benefit of hindsight, Tesla's eventual victory over the car dealers seems inevitable. Whatever the dealers' political power, whatever schemes they cooked up, whatever the equivocal support of GM and Ford, the dealers always had far more ways to lose than to win. As we'll see in Chapter 7, the politics of direct sales are complicated, but their arc bends toward freeing consumers to buy cars as they choose.

Notes

1. Brian Osborne, "Gateway Moves to 100% Indirect Distribution," Geek, July 28, 2008, https://web.archive.org/web/20151127170104/http://www.geek.com/chips/gateway-moves-to-100-indirect-distribution-576848/.
2. Mich. H. Legis. Analysis Section, Second Analysis, H.B. 4738, 4740, at 1 (1-26-99), www.legislature.mi.gov/documents/1997-1998/billanalysis/House/pdf/1997-HLA-4738-B.pdf.
3. Mich. H. Legis. Analysis Section, H.B. 5072 Synopsis (7-25-77).
4. H.B. 5606, 2014 Leg., Reg. Sess. (Mich. 2014), www.legislature.mi.gov/documents/2013-2014/billengrossed/House/pdf/2014-HEBS-5606.pdf.
5. Stephen Edelstein, "Michigan Car Dealers Slip One Over on Tesla, Ban Direct Sales: Updated," Green Car Reports, October 16, 2014, www.greencarreports.com/news/1094966_michigan-car-dealers-slip-one-over-on-tesla-ban-direct-sales.
6. Vince Bond Jr., "Anti-Tesla Bill Reaches Michigan Governor's Desk," Automotive News, October 15, 2014, www.autonews.com/article/20141015/RETAIL07/141019925/anti-tesla-bill-reaches-michigan-governor-s-desk/.
7. Greg Gardner, "Michigan Weighs Whether to Bar Tesla," USA Today, October 19, 2014, www.usatoday.com/story/money/cars/2014/10/19/michigan-tesla/17544663.
8. Ibid.
9. Justin Lloyd-Miller, "Tesla's Public Appeal Falls Short as Michigan Bans Direct Sales," Cheat Sheet: Autos, October 22, 2014, https://web.archive.org/web/20170428120953/ www.cheatsheet.com/automobiles/teslas-public-appeal-falls-short-as-michigan-bans-direct-sales.html/ ("We applaud Gov. Snyder's action of signing HB 5606. The bill will provide a level playing field for all automobile manufacturers selling vehicles in Michigan....") (quoting Ford)); Jared Meyer, "'Anti-Tesla Bill' Means Economic Loss for Michigan," Manhattan Institute, October 26, 2014, https://manhattan.institute/article/anti-tesla-bill-means-economic-loss-for-michigan-2 (reporting that both GM and Ford supported the Michigan bill); David Shepardson, "GM Backs Anti-Tesla Michigan Bill," The Detroit News, October 21, 2014,

www.detroitnews.com/story/business/autos/general-motors/2014/10/21/tesla-bill-michigan/17662581 ("We believe that House Bill 5606 will help ensure that all automotive manufacturers follow the same rules to operate in the State of Michigan; therefore, we encourage Governor Snyder to sign it…." (quoting GM)).

10. Letter from Rick Snyder, Governor, State of Michigan, to Michigan House of Representatives & Michigan Senate, October 21, 2014, www.michigan.gov/documents/snyder/HB_5606_Signing_Letter_472039_7.pdf.

11. Michael Wayland, "Tesla's Michigan Dealership Application at a Standstill," The Detroit News, May 12, 2016, www.detroitnews.com/story/business/2016/05/12/teslas-michigan-dealership-application-standstill/84267790/.

12. Greg Gardner, "Gov. Snyder Signs Bill Banning Direct Tesla Sales," Detroit Free Press, October 12, 2014, www.freep.com/story/money/cars/general-motors/2014/10/17/michigan-verge-banning-tesla-stores/17386251; Jeff Gilbert, "Governor Snyder Signs Michigan Tesla Ban," CBS News Detroit, October 21, 2014, http://detroit.cbslocal.com/2014/10/21/governor-signs-michigan-tesla-ban; Chris Isidore, "Tesla Blocked from Selling in Michigan," CNN Money, October 21, 2014, http://money.cnn.com/2014/10/21/news/companies/tesla-michigan; Micheline Maynard, "Michigan to Tesla Motors: You're Not Welcome," Forbes, October 21, 2014, www.forbes.com/sites/michelinemaynard/2014/10/21/michigan-to-tesla-motors-youre-not-welcome; Lucy Nicholson, "Michigan Becomes Fifth U.S. State to Thwart Direct Tesla Car Sales," Reuters, October 21, 2014, www.reuters.com/article/2014/10/21/us-tesla-motors-michigan-idUSKCN0IA2MR20141021; Robert Sorokanich, "GM Supports Anti-Tesla Bill in MI, Snyder Signs into Law," Road & Track, October 21, 2014, www.roadandtrack.com/car-culture/videos/a6309/michigan-governor-snyder-signs-gm-backed-anti-tesla-bill-into-law.

13. "Rick Snyder Drives off the Road: Michigan's Pro-Market Governor Embraces the Car Dealer Cartel," The Wall Street Journal, October 24, 2014, www.wsj.com/articles/rick-snyder-drives-off-the-road-1414192688.

14. Bob Sorokanich, "Gov. Snyder's Anti-Tesla Law Wins Michigan the 'Luddite Award'," Car & Driver, January 8, 2015, http://blog.caranddriver.com/gov-snyders-anti-tesla-law-wins-michigan-the-luddite-award.

15. Michael Wayland, "Tesla's Michigan Dealership Application at a Standstill," The Detroit News, May 12, 2016, www.detroitnews.com/story/business/2016/05/12/teslas-michigan-dealership-application-standstill/84267790/.

16. *Exxon Corp.* v. *Maryland*, 264 F 3d 493 (1978).

17. *Craigmiles* v. *Giles*, 312 F 3d 220 (6th Cir. 2002).

18. "Federal Judge Rules in Favor of Tesla: Michigan Lawmakers Must Surrender Records of Their Communications with 'Anti-Tesla' Lobbyists,"

Teslarati, August 22, 2017, www.teslarati.com/judge-tesla-lawsuit-michigan-lawmakers-surrender-communication-records/.
19. Ibid.
20. Joint Stipulation and Motion for Entry of Dismissal, *Tesla, Inc.* v. *Benson*, No. 16-cv-1158 (W.D. Mich. January 22, 2020), www.michigan.gov/ag/-/media/Project/Websites/AG/releases/2020/january/Joint_Stipulation_and_Motion_for_Entry_of_Dismissal_12220.pdf.
21. Motor Vehicle Franchise Act, H.B. 6233 (Mich. 2020), https://legislature.mi.gov/documents/2019-2020/billintroduced/House/pdf/2020-HIB-6233.pdf.

7 STRANGE BEDFELLOWS

During the first two decades of the twenty-first century, there were few more polarizing figures in America than Charles and David Koch, commonly known as the Koch Brothers. Two of the four sons of oil magnate Fred Koch, the Koch Brothers inherited a multi-billion-dollar energy empire that at times has ranked as the second-largest private business in America. While their father built a business empire, Charles and David built a political one. The Koch Brothers launched a massive effort to support conservative and libertarian causes, particularly those that sought to combat climate change, which the brothers denied was caused by human activity. Needless to say, the brothers had both their fans and their haters. When David died in 2019, *Jacobin* writer Branko Marcetic eulogized him as "an evil man who dedicated his life to evil."[1]

In addition to spending hundreds of millions of dollars to support Republican candidates for office, the brothers founded and funded the public interest organization Americans for Prosperity, which describes itself as a "grassroots organization that advocates for freedom and opportunity for all."[2] AFP works primarily to advance free-market, anti-regulatory, and anti-tax initiatives. In 2015, it lent its name and the Koch Brothers' cachet to Tesla's war against the car dealers. That led to some interesting news stories.

I had to suppress a laugh when my contact at the Sierra Club sheepishly asked whether I had planted the headline. There it was in black and white on Bloomberg: "Koch Brothers, Sierra Club Join Tesla in Fight With Dealers."[3] And there it was on Automotive News: "Tesla joined by Koch Brothers, Sierra Club in fight with dealers."[4]

Yahoo! similarly announced that the "Koch Brothers, Sierra Club Join Tesla Dealer Fight,"[5] the Denver Post had "Kochs, Sierra Club back Tesla,"[6] and many other national and local media outlets ran headlines to the same effect. Yes indeed, the environmentalist group Sierra Club and their sworn adversaries, the Koch Brothers' Americans for Prosperity, had joined forces in support of Tesla against the car dealers.

But had I planted the headline? To be sure, I had organized an advocacy letter on direct sales that had been joined by Americans for Prosperity and the Sierra Club with one another's knowledge, and also by a number of other environmentalist, free-market, and pro-consumer groups. And, yes, our goal was to get out the story of broad support for direct sales. And did it help spread the word that the Kochs and Sierra Club were singing from the same hymnal? Yes, it did. But had I planted the story? No, there were far too many headlines for me to have planted. Also, I didn't need to plant the story. Once our open letter went out, the story kind of planted itself.

My Sierra Club contact was fine with all of this. She was just checking in because, after the story broke, the Sierra Club got flak from some of its members. How could you ally yourself with those fossil-fuel-promoting, anti-environment, regressive Neanderthals? The simple answer was that the Sierra Club and Koch Brothers could disagree about 99 perfect of the issues and agree that state laws prohibiting direct sales were a bad idea. That they had entirely different reasons for this opinion did not detract from the bottom line. One general theme in the direct sales wars is that when you're the beneficiary of legal protectionism like the car dealers, you tend to find that lots of people who otherwise don't have much in common resent your special privileges. When you're in that position, your best hope may be that the people who resent your special privileges resent each other too much to do anything about it. That, at least, seems to be the dealers' best hope.

Tesla started out alone in the direct sales wars, but it wasn't long before it attracted a number of friends – environmentalists, technologists, consumer advocates, libertarians, civil rights groups, labor unions, and more. The strange bedfellows flocking to Tesla's banner had the makings of a formidable political coalition. They spanned the conventional political spectrum from left to right, covered core constituencies in both political parties, and could serve as a devastating riposte to the dealers' self-serving claims about why direct sales should be banned. When I speak with politicians or their aides, I typically point out that the direct sales issue has something for everyone. If you're a liberal Democrat, the environmentalist community will tell you that supporting direct sales is critical to flipping the fleet from internal combustion vehicles to EVs. If you're a conservative Republican, the free-market groups will tell you that the government shouldn't dictate to companies how to sell their cars. If you're somewhere in the middle, the consumer groups will tell you that allowing more flexibility in sales strategies creates more competition and consumer choice. And there simply is no significant ideological support for the car dealers' position. Climb aboard the bandwagon!

But of course it's not that simple. As we'll see in this chapter, ideology, policy, and politics are very different things. The ideological and policy positions happen to be fairly straightforward. Almost all of the varied public interest organizations that have taken an interest in direct sales support Tesla and the other electric vehicle (EV) start-ups. But politics is much more complicated. As we saw in Chapter 6 with the Michigan story, politicians follow many other things other than their stated ideology. Money is a big factor, of course, and the car dealers splash plenty of it. But there are also more intangible factors like history, relationships, and personality. On the latter point, there are few more polarizing figures in America today than Elon Musk. As we will see, his centrality to the direct sales story has complicated the narrative.

Let's start with the relatively simpler part of the story – ideology and policy. On April 14, 2021, a coalition of about thirty national and regional public interest organizations released an open letter supporting direct sales.[7] As with other open letters I'd helped to organize, the signatories' "individual interests include[d] such diverse matters as environmental protection, fair competition, consumer protection, economic growth and workforce development, and technology and innovation." They noted that "[s]ome of us frequently find ourselves on different sides of public policy debates." But the groups were willing to put aside their differences and "find common ground on an issue of considerable public importance concerning sales of electric vehicles ('EVs')." Specifically, they urged "that any state laws still prohibiting car companies from selling their cars directly to consumers, or opening service centers for those vehicles, be amended to permit direct sales and service of EVs." The coalition managed to agree that the direct sales prohibitions had five pernicious effects:

> (1) slowing the market penetration of EVs; (2) correspondingly, maintaining a higher share of internal combustion vehicles on the roads, with negative environmental consequences and prolonging singular dependence on petroleum fuels in transportation; (3) interfering with manufacturers' freedom to experiment with new distribution models for new technologies and market conditions, thus reducing the competitiveness of the U.S. EV industry and advantaging foreign competitors; (4) interfering with consumers' freedom to decide how they will purchase cars; and (5) interfering with free markets to privilege economic special interests.

Getting such a broad and diverse coalition to agree to just that was a good day's work!

Let's now take a look at the different interests in the coalition. The environmentalists' support has been rock-solid. The environmentalist groups supporting EV direct sales have included the American Council for an Energy-Efficient Economy, CALSTART, Environment America, the Sierra Club, Plug In America, the Acadia Center, the Alliance for Clean Energy New York, Connecticut League of Conservation Voters, Michigan Conservation Voters, New York League of Conservation Voters, Save the Sound, and many state chapters of the Public Interest Research Group. To the environmentalists, the case for direct sales of EVs is clear. According to the Department of Energy, "in 2023, U.S. motor gasoline and diesel (distillate) fuel consumption in the U.S. transportation sector accounted for about 31% [1,489 million metric tons (MMmt)] of total U.S. energy-related carbon dioxide (CO_2) emissions (4,794 MMmt)."[8] According to the Environmental Protection Agency, a typical internal combustion car emits 4.6 metric tons of carbon dioxide per year.[9] Internal combustion vehicles therefore are major contributors to carbon emissions, global warming, and climate change.

EVs are certainly not free of environmental hazards. They take energy to run too, and mining of lithium and other minerals necessary for batteries has its own negative consequences. But the Environmental Protection Agency (EPA) insists that EVs are "typically responsible for lower levels of greenhouse gases (GHGs) than an average new gasoline car," and that "[t]o the extent that more renewable energy sources like wind and solar are used to generate electricity, the total GHGs associated with EVs could be even lower."[10] This is politically contested territory (that the Trump Administration is likely to alter significantly), but there is no question that the environmentalist groups are all in on promoting the shift to EVs.

The environmentalist groups have also come to believe that a critical step to accelerating EV market penetration and flipping the fleet is to allow direct sales. The Sierra Club, in particular, has taken the lead in studying the inadequacies of the traditional franchised dealers when it comes to EV sales. As noted in Chapter 2, the Sierra Club has done secret shopper studies and other reports chronicling the dealers' unwillingness or incompetence when it comes to selling electric cars. One veteran environmentalist activist who works primarily in the South told me that, in his experience, it's not that the car dealers are unfamiliar with EVs. It's that they know all about them and hate the idea of having to sell them. The Sierra Club blames not only the dealers but also the legacy car manufacturers, noting in 2023 that "we are in a climate crisis and at a major inflection point for the American EV industry, and yet automakers are still pumping out millions of gas-powered vehicles while they lag on their EV commitments."[11] They have no such criticisms of EV start-ups like Tesla, Rivian, and Lucid, which sell only EVs and are pushing as hard as possible to sell more of them. For the environmentalists, joining forces with the EV start-ups on distribution comes naturally.

A second important building block of the coalition is the consumer groups. As we saw in Chapter 4, the consumer groups' support for direct sales is particularly significant because it counters the dealers' self-serving claims to represent consumer interests. Consumer groups that have joined the coalition supporting direct sales include the Consumer Federation of America, Consumer Action, and Consumers for Auto Reliability and Safety ("CARS"). As we have seen in earlier chapters, the Consumer Federation of America has been particularly critical of the car dealers' efforts to insulate themselves from direct sales competition, arguing that consumers don't like to haggle with car dealers and should have the choice of buying direct from the manufacturer for a one-size-fits-all price.

Free-market groups are another important part of the coalition. Groups that have joined the effort include Americans for Prosperity, R-Street, the Mackinac Center, the Institute for Justice, the Pelican Institute for Public Policy, and the libertarian-leaning International Center for Law and Economics. For libertarians and conservatives like the Koch Brothers, the case for allowing direct sales is straightforward. The state dealer franchise laws that dictate a distribution strategy to car companies get in the way of voluntary, contractual arrangements between manufacturers and consumers. There is no valid reason – such as the prevention of force or fraud – for such an interference in the market. If the dealers think they can offer value to manufacturers and consumers, let them make their case in the market, not in legislatures or courtrooms. Tesla played well to this theme, calling state laws that restricted its right to sell direct "an affront to the very concept of a free market."[12]

For the free market groups, there are two potential sticking points when it comes to direct sales. The first is the view that Tesla is no free-market white knight but rather the beneficiary of government subsidies and largesse. At the federal level, these include a 2010 $465 million preferential loan from the US Department of Energy and a federal EV tax credit of up to $7,500, which Elon Musk once dismissed as unnecessary but may be worth up to $42 billion to Tesla by the end of 2032.[13] Tesla has also made over half a billion dollars by selling environmental credits to other car companies, gotten a $1.3 billion tax break from the State of Nevada to build its gigafactory in Nevada,[14] and $64 million in tax breaks to build a gigafactory near Austin, Texas.[15] Libertarians sometimes sniff that, while they don't approve of the direct sales bans, they see no reason to expend effort to help a company that itself is the beneficiary of crony capitalism. In 2014, the conservative Mercatus Center agreed with Tesla that New Jersey's direct sales ban was "an affront to the very concept of a free market," but asserted that Tesla was getting a taste of its own medicine after years of playing crony capitalism over subsidies and tax breaks.[16] After joining the Sierra Club in supporting Tesla's right to sell direct in

2015, the Koch Brothers' Americans for Prosperity cooled off on the mission in 2018, arguing that "American taxpayers shouldn't have to subsidize luxury vehicles."[17]

To this argument I usually respond that the free-market groups are not being asked to support a company, but rather a free-market principle applicable to every company and to consumers who buy cars. If in their day jobs the libertarians want to fight tax credits, go for it. The coalition supporting direct sales has no dog in that fight. Many free-market groups respond positively to this perspective.

The other sticking point for some free-market groups is that the case for direct sales for EVs is too limited. They believe that there should be *no* restrictions on direct sales for *any* company, whether they sell EVs or gas-powered cars, and whether they have any franchised dealers or not. There are suspicions (evidenced by the presence of the environmentalist groups) that the coalition is trying to prop up EVs by giving them a competitive advantage over internal combustion cars. Why should EVs, or EV start-ups, get a special break?

As we'll see further in Chapter 6 of this book, the policy questions concerning competition and a level playing field between the legacies and start-ups are challenging. The case for allowing direct EV sales by any EV manufacturer is strong (although, as we saw in Chapter 5, General Motors (GM) has spurned the opportunity to pursue it). The harder case is whether, with the advent of EVs, the entire set of laws protecting dealers from their franchising manufacturers should be reconsidered. Some libertarians believe that these laws never had legitimate justifications and simply represented rent-seeking activity by small businesses during an era when "mom-and-pops" got a sympathetic ear in state legislatures. Others are willing to accept that the original laws may have had some justifications, but that (as discussed in Chapter 3), the economic circumstances of both the dealers and manufacturers have so changed that the laws need to be thrown out. And then there's the fact that some free market leaning groups and individuals are more conservative than libertarian. While they do not support government restrictions on distribution models in principle, they also are concerned about upending a longstanding legal framework, particularly when dealers have made significant investments in reliance on that legal framework.

Although no single answer will please everyone, the position advanced by the broad coalition – that any manufacturers selling EVs should be able to do so directly – has attracted considerable support from free-market groups. Whatever the history of the dealer franchise laws, and whatever reliance case the dealers may have based on those laws, there is no legitimate reason to block equal competition over a new technology by any company willing to make the investment. That is an argument that most committed libertarians and conservatives can get behind.

Many of the car dealers themselves feel conflicted about arguing that they should be protected from manufacturer competition even while trumpeting themselves as bastions of free market ideology. As we saw in Chapter 3, a few courageous dealers have defected from NADA's group think and said that Tesla should be allowed to do what it wants to do. But most continue to toe the party line, whatever their personal misgivings. A few years ago, I got a phone call from a Michigan car dealer who had read some of my public statements. He wanted to convince me that I was wrong. I said that I would be very happy to listen – go for it. He began his pitch by credentialing himself as a free-market conservative. But this is different, he pled. I waited to hear how it was different. After about a half hour's conversation, it appeared that the way it was different is that this time the money at issue was his. I tried to gently suggest that personal self-interest isn't a principled basis for regulations that restrict companies and consumers from making their own voluntary choices. When their own pocketbooks aren't at stake, free marketeers overwhelmingly support that message.

The triumvirate of environmentalist, consumer, and free-market groups makes up the core of the strange bedfellows coalition, but a number of diverse public interest groups have made significant contributions to the cause as well. The American Antitrust Institute ("AAI") – a leading organization of former government enforcers, academics, economists, and lawyers supporting more aggressive antitrust enforcement – joined the same open letter on direct sales as the Sierra Club and Americans for Prosperity. The AAI's endorsement underscores the point that the dealers are attempting to erect barriers that prevent effective competition in retail auto sales. The title of this book references the car dealers' monopoly. It is a monopoly on distribution methods that Tesla is challenging. Monopolies are costly to consumers, and they are costly to innovation.

Speaking of innovation, another organization that joined the direct sales effort is the Information Technology and Innovation Foundation ("ITIF"), which as we saw in Chapter 5 gave the State of Michigan a "Luddite award" for blocking Tesla. The ITIF's support underscores the fact that the dealers are not only attempting to block a new form of competition, but they are also really trying to block a new technology. When a new technology comes to market, its developers often need to invent a new way to market their product because existing distribution channels are closed. For example, in 1951, Timex entered the watch market to compete against the traditional hegemony of Swiss watchmakers.[18] Timex watches, manufactured from hard metal alloys, were made to be stylish and durable yet inexpensive. Traditional jewelry stores – the incumbent distribution channel for watches – were reluctant to carry the Timex brand because they offered slim margins and "the watches' riveted cases could not be opened, thereby eliminating the possibility for jewelers to generate aftersales repair revenues."[19] Accordingly, "Timex had no choice but to innovate in its marketing and distribution strategy."[20] It did so by eschewing jewelry stores in favor of "drugstores, discount houses, department stores, catalogue showrooms, military bases and sporting goods outlets."[21] If Timex had been forced to sell through jewelry stores, its innovative technology would not have come to market. So too with Tesla. Forcing Tesla to sell through established car distribution channels would not only deprive consumers of the choice of how to buy cars, it would effectively block many of them from accessing a new technology. And that, in turn, would make it difficult for the technology to reach scale and advance in development.

Another perspective in the Tesla wars is that of energy independence. The mission of Securing America's Future Energy ("SAFE") is "to improve America's energy security by significantly curtailing our dependence on oil and promoting responsible use of our domestic energy resources."[22] SAFE joined the direct sales coalition out of the apparent conviction that direct sales are important to EV market penetration and that moving toward EVs is strategically important to

America's security interest because EVs can be powered by domestically available energy sources.

As discussed in Chapter 6, the labor unions have not shown much of an interest in the direct sales issue, with the United Auto Workers union making a brief foray against the Michigan dealers when they tried to pass a law freezing a special privilege for Tesla. But two chapters of the International Brotherhood of Electrical Workers (IBEW) joined the big tent coalition letter supporting direct sales. More EVs means more work for electricians, and direct sales means more EVs.

I was particularly gratified when EVHybridNoire joined the coalition. EVHybridNoire describes itself as "the nation's largest network of diverse electric vehicle (EV) drivers and enthusiasts."[23] It "engage[s] with communities often left out of e-mobility discussions, advocate[s] for e-mobility solutions in underserved communities, and work[s] to shift the e-mobility narrative to include diverse populations." There are plenty of reasons for racial minorities and disadvantaged communities to oppose laws that restrict direct sales of EVs. As EVHybridNoire notes, "Black individuals were 42 percent more likely than white individuals to have asthma in the U.S." The African American community therefore stands to make significant health gains from a transition to EVs. Also, as noted in Chapter 5, the haggling-based model of dealer sales has not been kind to racial minorities. The flat-pricing model of company sales could shift the needle toward more equitable car purchasing and financing practices.

All told, the coalition of public interest organizations supporting direct sales spans a broad variety of groups that seldom, if ever, work together. What other cause attracts environmentalists, consumers, free market, antitrust, pro-technology, energy independence, labor, and equitable access groups to the same table? What other cause attracts that kind of coalition and faces no ideological counterweight on the other side, apart from a self-serving special interest? If a new lobbyist for one of the EV companies asked "who's on our side" and "who's on their side" and were furnished the list of direct sales allies and no list of direct sales opponents, her jaw would drop to the ground. She would surely think (although she surely wouldn't ask), "why do you need me?" The answer is that, while the case for direct sales is clear as

Strange Bedfellows 115

a matter of *policy*, it's much murkier as a matter of *politics*. To see why, let's take a jaundiced look at the crass red state/blue state facts.

Are red states or blue states more open to direct sales? That turns out to be a more complicated question than you might expect. As we'll see in Chapter 9, whether a state is "open" or "closed" to direct sales depends not only on when you ask that question – given the ongoing skirmishing in the Tesla wars that's a moving target – but also on how you measure what it means to be open or closed. But, as a rough approximation as of 2024, the map tells a story with a tilt. Among the "blue states," New York and Connecticut are outliers in banning direct sales. (New York legislation in 2014 allowed Tesla to keep its five existing stores but banned new ones.) Apart from that, the Northeast and Mountain and Pacific West – core "blue" territory – are mostly open for business. Meanwhile, many of the red states in the Plains and South – including Texas, Louisiana, Alabama, South Carolina, Mississippi, Arkansas, and West Virginia in the South alone – have said no to direct sales. Apparently, they missed the memo from the free-market organizations.

Among Republican elites, there has been some tepid interest in signaling a commitment to Tesla's right to sell direct. Various of the sometime presidential candidates have weighed in on the issue, generally advocating direct sales as a free market issue. In 2014, Florida Senator (now Secretary of State) Marco Rubio distinguished himself from his sometime rival New Jersey governor Chris Christie by questioning why Christie would block Tesla from selling in New Jersey.[24] Rubio argued that "[c]ustomers should be allowed to buy products that fit their need, especially a product that we know is safe and has consumer confidence beneath it" and that "regulations should never be used as a defensive weapon by an established industry or an established company." As we saw in Chapter 3, Christie quickly abandoned course and signed legislation allowing Tesla to operate in New Jersey. Meanwhile, another sometime GOP presidential candidate, Texas Governor Rick Perry, turned on the dealers, arguing that "[t]hese are old laws that have been put in place, and I am not going to argue whether they were right or wrong for then … but we live in a different world than we did 10 years ago."[25] In the early years of the Tesla wars, it seemed that the leadership of the Republican Party might be ready to lead the rank and file into a position more consistent with the party's free-market values.

Donald Trump popped that balloon. Although Trump has never publicly weighed in on the direct sales controversy, his MAGA brand of Republicanism marks a sharp departure from the neoconservative free-market ideology of the party intelligentsia and think tanks. Trump supports tariffs and oil, and disdains EVs. He has said that the Biden Administration's pro-EV policies will lead to a "bloodbath" in the US economy, "kill" the auto industry, and trigger an "assassination" of auto industry jobs.[26] He has pledged to end Biden policies aimed at promoting EV adoption. Apart from his rapprochement with Elon Musk (about which more in a moment), it's hard to imagine another Trump Administration leaning hard into the direct sales issues.

And then there is the abundant evidence that, whatever its free-market principles, the GOP remains tightly connected to the car dealers. As we saw in Chapter 3, the car dealers give a lot of money to political campaigns, and those donations lean heavily Republican. In 2009, statistician superstar Nate Silver found that 88 perfect of political contributions by car dealers went to Republicans, compared to 12 perfect to Democrats.[27] Silver argued that this shouldn't be a surprise. Car dealers "are usually male, they are usually older (you don't own an auto dealership in your 20s), and they have obvious reasons to be pro-business, pro-tax cut, anti-green energy and anti-labor." Further, "[c]ar dealerships need quite a bit of space and will tend to be located in suburban or rural areas. I can't think of too many other occupations that are more natural fits for the Republican Party. Unfortunately, while we are still a nation of drivers, we are not a nation of dealers."

What was true in 2009 remains true a decade and a half later. In May 2023, Slate journalist Alexander Sammon crashed NADA's national convention in Dallas, which was to be headlined by another star of the Republican Party, Trump's chief 2024 rival Nikki Haley.[28] Amid "flowing" booze, "open bars number[ing] in the double digits," "metal bathtubs teem[ing] with beer on ice," "line dancing and trick ropers, twirling lassos and mechanical bulls, bucking riders and stilt-walkers," Sammon found the heart of the Republican party. He concluded that "[a]lthough dealers are maligned as parasites, their relationship to the GOP is pure symbiosis: Republicans need their money and networks, and dealers need politicians to protect them from repealing the laws that keep the money coming in."

The GOP's ongoing alignment with a special interest group deeply mistrusted by a substantial majority of Americans suggests an opening for the Democrats to score political points on the direct sales issue. But while some have done that, few high-profile Democrats have seen fit to make direct sales a signature issue. Indeed, the strategy among many elite Democrats has been to avoid the direct sales issue as much as possible. During Barack Obama's second term as President, the White House promised that any petition that received 100,000 signatures within thirty days would receive an official response from the administration (upping the signature requirement from 25,000 in response to petitions like one for the United States to build a Death Star). In 2013, a petition to allow Tesla to sell direct got over 200,000 signatures. The Obama White House took over a year to respond, and its answer left few outside of NADA satisfied: "As you know, laws regulating auto sales are issues that have traditionally sat with lawmakers at the state level. We understand that pre-empting current state laws on direct-to-consumer auto sales would require an act of Congress."

That was a total dodge. While it's true that car sales have traditionally been regulated by states rather than the federal government, the executive branch of the federal government has no shortage of available tools through the Departments of Justice, Energy, Transportation, and the EPA and Federal Trade Commission to encourage states to open up competition in retail sales of automobiles. To the point that federal action would require an act of Congress, might the White House take a leadership role in promoting federal legislation? Have you heard of Obamacare? And even if the White House wasn't prepared to take direct political action on car distribution, it could easily have led a cheerleading effort against the car dealers' efforts to block direct sales, which would have certainly had an impact in the state-by-state battles. Instead, Obama officials decided to sit it out.

The Biden Administration seems to have followed the same path. It announced aggressive plans to boost EV sales – EV charger and vehicle tax credits, billions of dollars in grants to support public charging stations, hundreds of millions of dollars to support EV research and development, and grants to schools to purchase clean buses, among many other initiatives.[29] But not a word about an issue identified as critical to EV market penetration by the Administration's allies in the environmentalist community. This was not an oversight. The direct sales issue frequently makes national headlines, and environmentalists have pointedly raised it with the Administration. Like the Obama Administration, the Biden Administration showed little interest in engaging.

So here you have the oddity that public interest groups at the heart of both political parties have uniformly come out in favor of direct sales, but neither political party has shown any interest in engaging with the issue at a national level. Is it because the public isn't interested? The Obama White House petition suggests that isn't true. Is it because the public is ambivalent on whether direct sales should be allowed? Hardly. This is anecdotal, but whenever there's a major news story about direct sales on a site that allows readers to comment, I scan the comments and find that they overwhelmingly support direct sales. But don't take my word for it. In 2022, the Electrification Coalition commissioned New Bridge Strategy to conduct a poll on the issue in North Carolina.[30] New Bridge completed 600 interviews among North Carolina voters statewide. The pollsters explained that "under North Carolina law, consumers cannot buy a new vehicle straight from a manufacturer" but "instead, consumers have to buy a new vehicle through a franchised auto dealership, which is a separate, thirdparty company." They asked: "Would you support or oppose allowing North Carolina drivers to purchase a vehicle straight from the manufacturer, and to receive routine service and repairs on a vehicle from the manufacturer, without having to go through a dealership?" Fully 83 perfect of respondents supported direct sales, with 48 perfect "strongly" supporting it. This included 80 perfect of Republicans, 91 perfect of Independents, and 78 perfect of Democrats; 87 perfect of men and 80 perfect of women; 83 perfect of voters under age 45, 90 perfect of voters age 45–64, and 75 perfect of voters ages 65 and over. After hearing that "80 perfect of electric vehicles in the U.S. are purchased directly from the manufacturer," but that EV manufacturers other than Tesla were prohibited from direct sales, support for direct sales increased even further, even among voters with a negative view of EVs.

In this day and age, it's hard to think that a candidate or elected official from either party who decided to invest in the direct sales issue wouldn't be able to score some points with the public. To be sure, that would require explaining the issue clearly (and that's not always easy) and would bring on the wrath of the car dealers. But politicians from both parties have shown no fear about taking on even more powerful and less despised business interests like Google, Facebook, Apple, and Amazon, not to mention Big Oil, cable companies, and the news media. Is there really no political appetite to take on the car dealers in twenty-first-century America?

There are many possible explanations for both parties' vague avoidance of the direct sales issue, and no single explanation captures it all. Maybe the Democrats really do think that this issue is best decided at the state level. Maybe the Republicans really remain captured by the car dealers, whatever their free-market ideology. Maybe I've drunk the Kool Aid too long and direct sales just isn't that interesting or important an issue. Maybe, but there's one other overriding factor that deserves consideration as throwing a wrench into the red/blue narrative on direct sales: the person of Elon Musk.

Historians often debate whether individual men and women matter that much to history. Anyone who has slogged their way through *War and Peace* may remember that Leo Tolstoy devotes endless pages at the end of the novel to debunking the "great man" theory of history and asserting that the significance of any individual is imaginary. I don't want to come under criticism for attributing too much importance to Musk individually in the broad sweep of the Tesla wars. But, then again, we are talking about Elon Musk, one of the most brilliant, fascinating, unpredictable, infuriating, and polarizing figures ever to walk the planet. (If you doubt the polarizing point, just watch any You Tube video on people's reactions to the Cyber Truck.) Tolstoy be damned, I'm going with "Musk made a difference."

In Chapter 3, we saw how Musk quickly got into a war of words with Chris Christie, uncharacteristic of a billionaire tech magnate and CEO trying to sell a new product. But there's very little about Musk that isn't uncharacteristic of a billionaire tech magnate and CEO. He smokes pot on live TV, talks openly about his drug and sleeping habits, dates his subordinates, talks about sending people on a one-way trip to Mars, moves his company headquarters around like chess pawns in a culture war, and wages battles with a list of adversaries too long to list, but that should include at least the Securities and Exchange Commission, Bernie Sanders, Elizabeth Warren, Joe Biden, Jeff Bezos, advertisers for a business he just purchased (he told X advertisers to "go fuck themselves"),[31] the LGBT community, the nation of Ukraine, the entire State of California (which has slightly more people than Ukraine), and, most recently as of this book's publication, Donald Trump.

The problem with analyzing Musk's impact on the direct sales wars is not to prove that he had one – how could he not – but identifying exactly how it cut. In the early years of Tesla, Musk was polarizing as a business personality, but stayed out of politics. He was not only a darling to the environmentalist and tech communities but also topped the richest people in the world lists and therefore roused suspicions on the anti-corporate left. On the right, he was suspected as another "Left Coast elite," and of course hated by the Republican-leaning car dealers. (As Slate reported following the 2023 NADA convention, that much had not changed in 2023, even after Musk became a hero on the right.)[32] Over time, as Musk began to become culturally aligned with conservative causes and the Republican Party, the environmentalists found it harder to sell Tesla to their natural allies on the left. After Musk tweeted that Biden is "a damp sock puppet in human form,"[33] the left's alliance with Musk seemed formally over. In 2024, Connecticut State Representative Aimee Berger-Girvalo probably spoke for many Democrats when she said: "Since Elon Musk started to align himself with extreme authoritarian values, some Democrats who were for direct sales have dropped off. There's less support because association with Elon is a huge non-starter for many Democrats. I know I don't want to give a penny to Elon Musk."[34] Meanwhile, after he allied himself with the MAGA right by purchasing Twitter and pledging millions of dollars to Donald Trump's election campaign in 2024, Musk became a hero to conservatives as a person, but that did not necessarily translate into support for EVs. With Donald Trump deriding EVs and shouting "drill, baby, drill" at the RNC convention, what self-respecting MAGA supporter would pull out in a Tesla?

Except that, again, these things are complicated. In 2022, Democrats made up 40 perfect of Tesla customers.[35] By 2024, Democrats were abandoning the Tesla brand in droves, falling to only 15 perfect of Tesla's purchasers. Republicans (32 perfect) and Independents (44 perfect) took up most of the slack, although Tesla sales also fell for the first time. Could the now-fading bromance between Trump and Musk lower the right's aversion to EVs, turn Tesla into a Republican brand like Cadillac used to be, and finally lead to the MAGA crowd squarely coming out in support of direct sales consistent with the party's nominal attachment to deregulation and free markets?

The ultimate effect on Tesla and the direct sales wars from Trump and Musk's relationship remains to be seen. At the time I completed this book in early 2025, Trump and Musk seemed to be at the height of their alliance, with Musk heading Trump's Department of Government Efficiency ("DOGE") and Trump buying a Tesla from Musk at a White House event. Then, in the Spring of 2025, after Trump proposed to eliminate EV tax credits, the Trump-Musk relationship went into a freefall, with Musk going so far as to claim on X that Trump was in the notorious "Epstein files" (a thinly veiled accusation that Trump was a sexual predator). The two seemed to dial down their drama in subsequent weeks, but their future relationship, and its potential effects on the direct sales issue, remains highly unpredictable.

As we look forward to the shifting ideological alignments and politics of the direct sales wars, any number of scenarios are plausible. Looking back, we can say at least this. The first decade of the Tesla wars was marked by a fascinating set of strange bedfellows: ideological groups lining up to support direct sales, only to meet an equivocal response by both major political parties. I won't say that this episode is unparalleled in American history, but it certainly is remarkable, and will merit careful study by historians once the dust settles.

Elon Musk and Tesla have taken center stage in this story, but as the second decade of the Tesla wars emerges, we should maybe stop referring to them as the Tesla wars. As we'll see in Chapter 9, Tesla had won most of its major battles by the early years of the Biden Administration, but a whole new crop of EV start-ups had come along. As we'll see in Chapter 8, Tesla had both paved the way for the EV start-ups behind it, and also left behind some speed bumps for them to navigate.

Notes

1. Branko Marcetic, "For Humanity, David Koch Died Decades Too Late," Jacobin, August 23, 2019, https://jacobin.com/2019/08/david-koch-obituary-billionaire-evil.
2. Americans for Prosperity, https://americansforprosperity.org/.
3. Dana Hull, "Koch Brothers, Sierra Club Join Tesla in Fight with Dealers," Bloomberg, February 17, 2015, www.bloomberg.com/news/articles/2015-02-17/koch-brothers-sierra-club-join-tesla-in-fight-with-dealers.
4. Dana Hull, "Tesla Joined by Koch Brothers, Sierra Club in Fight with Dealers," Automotive News, February 17, 2015, www.autonews.com/article/20150217/RETAIL07/150219846/tesla-joined-by-koch-brothers-sierra-club-in-fight-with-dealers.
5. "Koch Brothers, Sierra Club Join Tesla Dealer Fight," yahoo! finance, February 17, 2025, https://finance.yahoo.com/video/koch-brothers-sierra-club-join-205835165.html.
6. "Kochs, Sierra Club back Tesla Motors," The Denver Post, February 17, 2015, www.denverpost.com/2015/02/17/kochs-sierra-club-back-tesla-motors/.
7. "Open Letter by Public Interest Organizations in Favor of Direct EV Sales and Service," April 14, 2021, https://laweconcenter.org/wp-content/uploads/2021/04/Direct-Sales-Nationwide-Organizations-Open-Letter-4.13.pdf.
8. "Frequently Asked Questions (FAQs)," US Energy Information Administration, www.eia.gov/tools/faqs/faq.php?id=307&t=10#:~:text=CO%202%20emissions%20from%20motor,related%20carbon%20CO%202%20emissions (last updated April 30, 2024).
9. "Greenhouse Gas Emissions from a Typical Passenger Vehicle," US Environmental Protection Agency, www.epa.gov/greenvehicles/greenhouse-gas-emissions-typical-passenger-vehicle (last updated August 23, 2024).
10. "Electric Vehicle Myths," US Environmental Protection Agency, www.epa.gov/greenvehicles/electric-vehicle-myths (last updated January 23, 2025).
11. Larisa Manescu, "Sierra Club Releases Nationwide Investigation into Electric Vehicle Shopping Experience," Sierra Club, May 8, 2023, www.sierraclub.org/press-releases/2023/05/sierra-club-releases-nationwide-investigation-electric-vehicle-shopping.
12. Matthew D. Mitchell, "Tesla Learns the Hard Way about Crony Capitalism's Downside," Mercatus Center, March 21, 2014, www.mercatus.org/economic-insights/expert-commentary/tesla-learns-hard-way-about-crony-capitalisms-downside.

13. Kate Aronoff, "Tesla Subsidies Are Cheaper Now, Thanks to Subsidies Musk Once Hated," New Republic, September 7, 2023, https://newrepublic.com/article/175397/teslas-cheaper-now-thanks-subsidies-musk-hated.
14. Jason Lalljee, "Elon Musk Is Speaking Out against Government Subsidies. Here's a List of the Billions of Dollars His Businesses Have Received," Business Insider, December 15, 2021, www.businessinsider.com/elon-musk-list-government-subsidies-tesla-billions-spacex-solarcity-2021-12.
15. Isabelle Gius, *Tax Breaks Cushion Tesla's Texas Landing*, The American Prospect (April 25, 2022) https://prospect.org/economy/tax-breaks-cushion-teslas-texas-landing/.
16. Matthew D. Mitchell, "Tesla Learns the Hard Way about Crony Capitalism's Downside," Mercatus Center, March 21, 2014, www.mercatus.org/economic-insights/expert-commentary/tesla-learns-hard-way-about-crony-capitalisms-downside.
17. Martin Rodriguez, "ICYMI: American Taxpayers Shouldn't Have to Subsidize Luxury Vehicles," Americans for Prosperity, October 9, 2018, https://americansforprosperity.org/press-release/icymi-tesla-drivers-dont-need-taxpayer-handouts/.
18. David W. Conklin, *Cases in the Environment of Business: International Perspectives* (Thousand Oaks, CA: Sage Publications, 2006), p. 53.
19. Ibid.
20. Ibid.
21. Ibid.
22. "Unleashing American Energy Dominance for National and Economic Security: About SAFE," SAFE, https://secureenergy.org/about/ (last visited February 15, 2025)
23. "Our Story," EVHybridNoire, https://evhybridnoire.com/our-story/ (last visited February 15, 2025)
24. Jeff Morganteen, "Sen Rubio: Allow Tesla to Sell Direct to Consumers," CNBC, March 25, 2014, www.cnbc.com/2014/03/25/sen-rubio-allow-tesla-to-sell-direct-to-consumers.html.
25. Charles Morris, "Tide Turning for Tesla in Texas? Governor Perry Favors Direct Sales," Charged, March 26, 2014, https://chargedevs.com/newswire/tide-turning-for-tesla-in-texas-governor-perry-favors-direct-sales/.
26. Allan Smith, "With Violent Rhetoric, Trump Fights Electric Vehicles to Defeat Biden in Michigan," NBC News, April 9, 2024, www.nbcnews.com/politics/2024-election/trump-fights-electric-vehicles-defeat-biden-michigan-violent-rhetoric-rcna145689.
27. Nate Silver, "News Flash: Car Dealers Are Republicans (It's Called a Control Group, People)," FiveThirtyEight: Politics, May 27, 2009, http://fivethirtyeight.com/features/news-flash-car-dealers-are-republicans.
28. Alexander Sammon, "Want to Stare Into the Republican Soul in 2023?," Slate, May 20, 2023, https://slate.com/news-and-politics/2023/05/rich-republicans-party-car-dealers-2024-desantis.html.

29. "FACT SHEET: Biden-Harris Administration Announces New Actions to Cut Electric Vehicles Costs for Americans and Continue Building Out a Convenient, Reliable, Made-in-America EV Charging Network," The American Presidency Project, January 19, 2024, www.presidency.ucsb.edu/documents/fact-sheet-biden-harris-administration-announces-new-actions-cut-electric-vehicle-costs.
30. "North Carolina Voters Support Direct Vehicle Sales," New Bridge Strategy, May 17, 2022, https://electrificationcoalition.org/wp-content/uploads/2022/08/NC-Key-Findings-Memo-d1b.pdf.
31. Colette Bennett, "One of Elon Musk's Businesses Has a Powerful New Enemy," The Street, December 13, 2023, www.thestreet.com/technology/one-of-elon-musks-businesses-has-a-powerful-new-enemy-.
32. Alexander Sammon, "Want to Stare Into the Republican Soul in 2023?," Slate, May 20, 2023, https://slate.com/news-and-politics/2023/05/rich-republicans-party-car-dealers-2024-desantis.html.
33. Chris Isidore, "Tesla Owners Are More Republican than You'd Think," CNN, February 3, 2022, www.cnn.com/2022/02/03/cars/tesla-buyer-politics/index.html.
34. Jim Motovalli, "Tesla's Evolving Direct Sales Battle – And the Elon Musk Factor," Autoweek, July 16, 2024, www.autoweek.com/news/a61612955/teslas-direct-sales-battle-elon-musk-connecticut/.
35. Tim Higgins, "Elon Musk Lost Democrats on Tesla When He Needed Them Most," The Wall Street Journal, April 20, 2024, www.wsj.com/business/autos/elon-musk-turned-democrats-off-tesla-when-he-needed-them-most-176023af.

8 THE OTHERS

RJ Scaringe grew up in Florida near the Indian River. A car enthusiast and the son of an engineer, the young RJ grew up tinkering with cars in his neighbor's garage. But like many teenagers in the 1990s, RJ began to feel guilty about his love of internal combustion engines.[1] As he would later put it, "I started to realize that vehicles are at the center of so many of the challenges we have – local air quality, climate change. And I became really bummed that these things I loved are such a source of problems for our planet."[2]

Fortunately, when an engineer sees a problem, his disposition is not to complain about it but to try and fix it. And so RJ, the environmentalist-engineer, set out to create a company that would make cars that could co-exist with nature. To meet Scaringe's vision, these cars would have to be both electric and rugged. To make money, they would have to appeal to the environmentally conscious, granola-eating, affluent crowd that likes to imagine itself storming rocky craigs while shuttling the kids to the soccer game. (I'm not making fun – did I mention that I drive a Subaru?) And the company would need an evocative name. Casting back to his childhood on the Indian River, Scaringe came up with one: *Rivian*.

Of course, by the time that RJ Scaringe got going with Rivian, Elon Musk had a big head start with Tesla. How would that shake out for Rivian? People who study business and technology sometimes wonder whether it's better to go first or second. Is there a first-mover advantage or a first-mover *disadvantage*? The first company to bring a new technology to market may obtain significant advantages over later comers. It may secure twenty-year patents, lock up key resources, establish brand loyalty with customers, get a head start on the competition, and set expectations, terms of dealing, and technological infrastructure to its own benefit. But there are also advantages to going second or even a little later. The first company has to expend major resources to figure things out, prove the concept, establish customer acceptance, and navigate the rocky shoals of law and regulation. Later comers can copy the first company's successes and avoid its mistakes. Google wasn't the first search engine to market. Remember Northern Light, Altavista, Magellan, and Yahoo? Me neither.

Tesla was the first mass-market electric vehicle (EV) company, and by a wide margin. Its success opened a door that many other companies like RJ Scaringe's Rivian are trying to drive through. Many of those companies will barely get through the door. Like in the early days of the automobile industry, many will be called, but few will be chosen. There is no guarantee that Tesla itself will be a survivor in this dog-eat-dog market.

It is still early days for the others drafting behind Tesla (though some have already come and gone). Many different factors will decide their success or failure. Of those, state laws regulating how cars are sold and serviced are just one, but they are not insignificant. The companies that came behind Tesla benefitted immensely from Tesla's fight to secure the right to sell direct. It is doubtful that many of them would have had the resources or stamina to battle the car dealers' powerful lobby across the nation, in the way that Tesla did behind the pocketbook and pugnaciousness of its mercurial leader. On the other hand, Tesla's victories in the car dealer wars did not leave a uniformly smooth road for its successors. As we'll see, Tesla sometimes won in ways that seemed to bar anyone else from following.

The story of the others isn't just about how the others were helped or hurt by Tesla's trailblazing on direct sales. It's also about how each successive entrant added some additional color to the arguments over the dealer franchise laws. To get at these stories, we'll begin by introducing some of the other companies – big and small, successful or unsuccessful – that tried to ride Tesla's wake. We'll then examine some of the legal, regulatory, and political implications of following in Tesla's wake.

In the early days of the Tesla wars, when Tesla was the only EV start-up around and I wanted to make the case that "this isn't just about Tesla," my favorite example was a little company that didn't even sell EVs. In 2014, Elio Motors, an American start-up company based in Phoenix, Arizona, announced that it was in the process of mass-producing a three-wheeled, two-seated internal combustion vehicle that it said would sell for $6,800 and achieve 84 miles per gallon on the highway.[3] (I have to admit that, though I'm a motorcyclist, I was always terrified at thought of tooling around Hummers and Expeditions in Elio's mosquitoesque two-seater.) The company planned to manufacture its diminutive cars at a former General Motors (GM) plant in Shreveport, Louisiana. On its website, Elio proclaimed that it planned to open its own showrooms and pursue a direct distribution model: "We will not be selling franchises or dealerships. Our plan is to open 120 company owned retail centers in the top sixty markets in the US."[4] For service, the company planned to contract with Pep Boys.

At a 2016 FTC hearing on direct sales, the company explained its thinking.[5] Elio had calculated that, in order to offer customers vehicles with every possible combination of available features, they would have to keep 10,000 vehicles sitting around a lot. That wasn't viable, so Elio planned to manufacture individually customized and configured vehicles to a customer's specifications. Once a customer selected all of their desired specs, the order would be sent to one of seven marshalling centers, where inventory was waiting. The marshalling centers would remain open until midnight (retail stores until 9 pm), so final assembly could be quickly processed to spec on a regional basis, with the finished product delivered to Elio's retail centers by 10 am the next day. Next-day custom manufacturing, presto! Elio described itself as the "sub-four-minute mile of manufacturing."

Sound too good to be true? It was. After accepting tens of thousands of customer reservation deposits, Elio staggered along for the better part of a decade, occasionally promising new technological strategies, including, at one point, a shift to an electric motor. But no product was ever forthcoming. Wikipedia reports that in 2024 the Elio website disappeared and a "404 Not Found" error appeared. I lost contact with the company a long time ago and don't know much about its demise.

Despite Elio's demise, its presence in the early years of the direct sales wars helped to dispel the idea that allowing direct sales was just about feathering the pockets of Internet billionaires. In 2015, Elio launched a grassroots effort to change political attitudes on direct sales at the retail level in Michigan. The company reached out to the Republican Party County Chair in every Michigan county and explained the Elio story. A lobbyist for the company told me that the message "has been enthusiastically received, some of them venomously opposed to the direct sales ban, now that they hear the Elio story."

The car dealers probably wouldn't have cared very much if Elio did whatever it wanted, except for the precedent it would set for others. Their lobbyists are glad that it failed. But it would be a mistake to draw any significant lesson about the viability of direct sales as a business matter from the failure of Elio, or any other manufacturer. As noted in Chapter 1, between 1900 and 1920, over 600 separate companies attempted to produce and sell an internal combustion automobile, and only three of them emerged successful. Failure is written into the rules of the game. Elio never produced an actual car, and so never got to test its direct sales strategy. That's a shame. I have no idea whether Elio's distribution and service strategy would have worked, but it would have added to our collective stock of knowledge to see it tried. The franchise dealer laws prevent innovation in distribution methods. While that may prevent some companies from trying bad strategies, without experimentation we'll never learn about good strategies. Whatever else one can say about Elio, it should have had *the right to fail*.

Another company that drafted in Tesla's wake and cuts a very different figure than Elio is Rivian. Founded in 2009 by RJ Scaringe, the company develops its high-end EVs on a "skateboard" platform that can be adapted to multiple generations of EVs, or even used by other companies. Its first two vehicles – a full-size SUV called the R1S and a smallish pickup truck called the R1T – launched in the middle of COVID and the global chip shortage that forced long roll-out delays. The R1S hit the market in late 2021, with the R1S close behind. Rivian differentiates itself from Tesla along a number of different dimensions but competes head-to-head on what may be the most important competitive dimension of the early years of the EV – battery range. While most early EVs have batteries that promise little more than 200 miles between charges, Teslas and Rivians promise in the 300 and 400 mile range (whether they always deliver on that promise is another matter). For early EV adopters worried about finding a charging station during the next road trip, range is paramount.

Geographically, Rivian has taken migratory steps opposite to Tesla. Tesla was founded in California and then migrated toward the heartland, ending up headquartered in Austin, Texas. Rivian was initially headquartered in Plymouth, Michigan, and took over a former Mitsubishi manufacturing plant in Normal, Illinois. By 2020, it had migrated many of its operations to Irvine, California. It still has operations in Michigan, but never took on the mantle of a Michigan car company. Ford invested $500 million in Rivian in 2019, and the two companies announced plans for Ford to build a pickup truck on Rivian's platform. Ford cancelled those plans in 2021 when it created a separate business unit to make EVs. While Ford's investment in Rivian paid off in the stock market for a while, when Rivian's stock price declined precipitously in 2022 and 2023, Ford began to withdraw from the company, eventually taking a $7.3 million write-down on its Rivian investment in 2023. On the other hand, Volkswagen announced a $5.8 billion investment in Rivian in June 2024.

Outside of the Michigan car world, Rivian has found no shortage of well-heeled friends. It has announced partnerships with Mercedes and Volkswagen to develop and build EVs in Europe. Perhaps most significantly, Rivian has partnered with Amazon to build electric delivery vans ("EDVs") for the world's largest online retailer. The Wall Street Journal has aptly described the EDVs as having "soft, sad eyes that say, Please don't ticket me, officer."[6] It seems to be working. By 2023, 10,000 Rivian EDVs were delivering on Prime's two-day guarantee. Amazon has reportedly ordered 100,000 of the vehicles.

For now, Rivian is Tesla's closest competitor. In a world of innovators and mold-breakers, Rivian has been by far the more "normal" company, operating with neither the manic energy nor political drama surrounding Elon Musk and his companies. As the second in line, Rivian has had to take up much of the mantle on direct sales among the second-generation EV start-ups. Like Elio, it's been easier to sell Rivian than Tesla as the face of the direct sales movement. Unlike Elio,

Rivian has actually had a product that it needs to get to customers. The direct sales issues haven't been hypothetical but have been one of the company's most pressing and immediate business challenges.

Quite naturally, Rivian "poached" many employees from Tesla. None may have been more important than Jim Chen, who served for six years as Tesla's Director of Public Policy and Associate General Counsel before decamping for Rivian, where he served as Vice President of Public Policy and assumed responsibility for Rivian's entry into the direct sales wars. (Chen left Rivian in 2023.) Rivian realized early on that it would not simply be able to coast along behind Tesla, but that it would have to make its own case for the right to sell and service its own cars.

Much of the case Rivian made for direct sales mirrored the case laid out by Tesla in Chapter 2. Rivian stressed that "consumer education" was critical to the success of its business, and that "auto dealerships are not well equipped to provide this education and are reluctant to upgrade for EV infrastructure, due to the relatively small numbers of EVs currently in production."[7] It noted that "[r]emoving an intermediary from the sales process ensures cost savings for consumers."[8] And it echoed Tesla's arguments that "[d]ealerships generate over half of their revenue from servicing and maintenance of internal combustion equipped vehicles," and that "EVs, with fewer moving parts and almost zero routine maintenance requirements, do not serve this part of the dealership business model – disincentivizing franchise dealerships from selling electric vehicles."[9]

Rivian also made a new argument about the importance of direct sales for EV start-ups. Having spoken on many occasions with company personnel and been with Rivian when it testified at legislative hearings, I got the impression that this was the point that Rivian cared about the most. Rivian argued that the connectivity between customers and the company was critical to the success of the company's products and consumers' experience of them. Unlike with internal combustion cars, EVs were essentially computers on wheels: "[w]ith owner permission, EV manufacturers remain connected to the vehicle for over-the-air software and security upgrades, performance diagnostics, and more. Operating through a dealership precludes this, to the detriment of customer convenience and reliability."[10] For example, if a Rivian buyer opted in, Rivian would continuously monitor the vehicle's performance and give the owner real-time recommendations about getting the most out of their car and when service might be needed. In Rivian's view, this kind of a direct and ongoing relationship between company and customer started with a direct transaction in the purchase and servicing of the vehicle.

The car dealers contested Rivian's argument, saying that nothing in the franchised dealer sales model precluded an EV company from having this kind of relationship with customers. That position pretty quickly lost credibility when the car dealers started lobbying legislatures to prohibit manufacturers from doing over-the-air updates on their own cars. In February 2022, the dealers got a bill introduced into the West Virginia legislature that any entity other than a dealer from providing "post-sale software and hardware upgrades or changes to vehicle function and features."[11] Fortunately, the bill didn't pass. But it did reveal the dealers' mindset. They would fight technological changes to avoid being cut out of lucrative service transactions, even if that meant forcing customers to take time off work to visit a dealer to get a software update that could have been done while the customer was sleeping. Imagine if you had to take your iPhone to a service center every time Apple released a software update!

Rivian successfully made the point that EVs were brand-new technologies that differed in significant ways from internal combustion cars, and that this implied significant differences in how EVs needed to be sold. Their arguments resonated with people who didn't know much about car distribution because they related EVs to technologies that everyone used on a daily basis. Not everyone was sold on the idea of a car company continuously monitoring their car's behavior. It's a short jump from the car's behavior to *your* behavior. That said, most people could understand the importance of allowing people who wanted that kind of relationship with their car company to opt into it. And most people could also understand that it makes sense to start that kind of manufacturer-consumer connectivity with a direct sale from the manufacturer to the consumer.

Like most of the EV start-ups, Rivian's ride hasn't always been smooth. After the company went public in 2021, its stock reached a high of $172 a share, before falling as low as $8.40 in April 2024. The company had to apologize for retroactive price increases of 17% and 20% on the R1T and R1S, experienced the loss of many top executives in 2023 (including Jim Chen, who had guided Rivian's direct sales strategy), and laid off 10% of its salaried workforce in early 2024. As of this writing, however, the company's stock price has recovered to nearly $17 a share, it has announced ambitious plans for two new SUVs, and its Amazon delivery vans are all over town. It has stores or galleries in British Columbia, California, Colorado, Georgia, Illinois, New York, Tennessee, Texas, and Washington.[12] Most importantly for the direct sales battles, no dealer has ever sold or serviced one of its cars. If a Rivian needs service, the company brings the technician to the customer's house or place of business in one of its mobile service vehicles. And customers aren't complaining about their experience. In 2024, Consumer Reports rated Rivian number one in customer satisfaction, with a whopping 86% of customers saying they would buy one again (compared to Mini at a distant second with 77% of customers saying they would buy again).[13] Rivian has not only added to the policy arguments for direct sales, but it has also provided a new model of how a direct approach can be successful.

Rivian sells vehicles to both individual customers and fleets, but some EV start-ups focus only on fleet sales because they make vehicles that retail customers wouldn't buy. Arrival was such a company. Headquartered in Luxembourg with its research and development facilities in Oxfordshire in the UK, Arrival planned to make four lightweight electric commercial vehicles: a bus, a van, a large van, and a small vehicle platform. It planned to have a large presence in the United States.

Arrival joined the coalition advocating for direct sales in the United States and, together with the Electrification Coalition, helped to articulate a case for direct sales focused on fleet purchasers and operators as the customers.[14] It noted that many purchasers of buses and delivery vehicles are governments, so that taxpayers pay the bill if state laws force sales and servicing to occur through costly dealer networks. Some fleet purchasers, particularly those within governments, are required to buy from a particular list of dealers, which may exclude EV start-ups. These regulations place especially smaller fleets at the mercy of a few dealers and deny them the flexibility to negotiate for products and buying arrangements that best fit their needs. Arrival also noted that many franchise laws require the dealer to broker the financing of the sale and that dealership finance managers are compensated based on their ability to convince the customer to add on costly accessories and warranties to increase monthly payments and interest revenue to the dealership. It noted that EV-only manufacturers are uniquely positioned to offer online sales and financing for commercial customers, but many state franchise dealership laws prohibit them from doing so. Finally, Arrival pointed out that laws that restricted a manufacturer's ability to provide warranty service for its own vehicles were particularly pernicious as to commercial vehicles due to the lack of EV service centers and trained technicians for these vehicles.

Like Elio, Arrival wasn't meant to be (at least yet). After a series of layoffs, relocation plans, new partnerships, and strategic retooling, Arrival went into liquidation in 2024. While that particular company didn't succeed, the case it made for the distinctive importance of direct sales and service to fleet operators remains important. As other makers of light or heavy commercial vehicles transition toward EVs, or new companies enter the market, the flexibility to sell direct will be vital to them too.

After Rivian, the most active of the Tesla successors in the direct sales wars has been Newark, California-based Lucid Motors. Funded with the deep pockets of the sovereign wealth fund of Saudi Arabia, Vanguard Group, BlackRock, and State Street, Lucid appears to be aiming for the Lexus segment of the EV market. Its Lucid Air luxury car hit the streets in 2022, earning Motor Trend's Car of the Year (the first time a new car model from a new company ever won that award). Lucid's distinctive technological contribution has been a focus on battery range and performance, which has paid off as some of its models top 500 miles on a single charge.[15]

Like Tesla, Rivian, and the other EV start-ups, Lucid has taken the position that the freedom to sell and service its own cars is critical to its ability to compete. Also like Rivian, it's hired former Tesla employees to help make that pitch. But Lucid has distinguished itself from the pack by staking the most aggressive legal strategy against the direct sales laws. In 2022, Lucid filed a constitutional challenge to Texas's direct sales ban in federal court in Austin, naming officials of the Texas Department of Motor Vehicles as defendants.[16] To be sure, as we saw in Chapter 7, Tesla had filed a constitutional challenge to Michigan's direct sales ban that resulted in the settlement with the Attorney General that opened up Tesla's ability to sell and service its cars in Michigan. But the Tesla challenge was limited to the facts surrounding the 2014 legislation and Michigan's subsequent denial of Tesla's license applications. By contrast, Lucid went for the jugular, arguing that, as applied to EV-only manufacturers, the direct sales ban is "pure economic protectionism for the benefit of Texas's existing auto dealers" and that it is divorced from any legitimate state interest. It's a gamble, but if Lucid wins its case in the trial court and eventually the Fifth Circuit Court of Appeals, it will likely wipe away the remaining direct sales prohibitions in Texas, Louisiana, and Mississippi. If the case goes to the Supreme Court and Lucid wins, that could be the end of direct sales restrictions on EV-only manufacturers across the country.

Thus far, Lucid's on a good run in Austin. The district court denied the dealers' motion to dismiss the case, allowed the Texas Automobile Dealers Association to intervene in support of the ban (which I count as an unabashed win for *Lucid*), denied an early motion for summary judgment by Lucid without prejudice and only because it was premature, and denied the defendant's efforts to prohibit Professor Fiona Scott Morton, a distinguished Yale Management School Professor and former Chief Economist at the Justice Department's Antitrust Division, from testifying in favor of Lucid. Any hope the dealers had of giving the case the back of the hand based on constitutional principles allowing states latitude in economic regulation was quickly dashed. While the ultimate outcome of the case remains uncertain, Lucid's bold move showcases the importance of having multiple different companies, representing different perspectives and legal and business strategies, fighting the direct sales bans. While the story has often been painted as Tesla against the world, it's become much broader, more complicated, and even more interesting.

One of the more interesting EV start-ups is Scout Motors, which plans to roll out a pickup truck and an SUV from its Blythewood, South Carolina plant, with initial production targeted for 2027. American car enthusiasts may remember the original rugged Scout SUVs, built by

International Harvester between 1961 and 1980. They were the archetypes of a whole generation of SUVs to follow. In 2021, Volkswagen AG acquired the defunct Scout brand and re-launched the company as a new American brand whose EVs would faithfully reflect the design features of the original Scout vehicles. In February 2025, I met with Scout Motors CEO Scott Keogh at the company's R&D facility in Novi, Michigan. Mr. Keogh explained that Scout Motors sees direct sales and service of its vehicles as vital to the company's success. Among other reasons, Scout Motors' success will depend on the company nurturing direct relationships with its customers, both at the point of sale and service.

Many other EV start-ups have joined the direct sales cause as well. In Chapter 2, we saw that the reborn version of Fisker backed away from its earlier, unsuccessful strategy of dealer distribution and committed itself to direct sales before reversing itself again and then failing a second time. Faraday Future, named after English physicist Michael Faraday, who discovered electromagnetic induction, has struggled to get off the ground in Las Vegas, and may not make it. Nikola Motors – like Tesla named for the famous electrical engineer Nikola Tesla – identified direct sales prohibitions as a business risk factor in its 2020 IPO filing with the SEC.[17] This was not too long before Nikola's CEO was indicted for securities fraud. The company's still going, but obviously tarnished. Other small players seem to have a fair chance of making it. Aptera Motors, a crowd-funded, pre-production start-up company based in Carlsbad, California, is developing a two-seat, three-wheeled solar EV. The company has been adamant in its support for direct sales hiring lobbyists to make the case in Washington. Lordstown Motors planned to build an electric pickup truck at the former GM plant in Lordstown, Ohio. It has emerged from bankruptcy as Nu Ride and seems to be on the road again. Bollinger Motors planned to build an electric sport utility vehicle that will put Range Rovers to shame for pure safari appeal before shifting to a commercial vehicle platform. Like the others, it too has announced a direct sales strategy.

Others may come too, and it seems unlikely that many of them will opt to franchise dealers. You can call them Tesla copycats, but that's only half true. I've spent enough time talking to many of them to know that there are lots of different business models, technologies, personalities, and, yes, egos going on here. At some level, these companies are all in the same boat, but there are also fierce competitors. As between the car dealers and each other, it's not clear who they see as the greater enemy. If one of these companies sees a chance to break from the pack, sign up the dealers, and leapfrog the others, you can bet that they will. That hasn't happened yet (at least among U.S. EV start-ups), which is a testament to the fact that the arguments on the importance of direct sales are on to something.

Of course, Tesla's successors are copycats to the extent that they want to drive through the holes Tesla has made in the franchise dealer laws. In some states, that's possible. For example, as we saw in Chapter 6, the other EV start-ups have been able to take advantage of the favorable settlement that Tesla achieved in Michigan, which is not logically limited to Tesla (despite the dealers' efforts to make it so by statute). In other states, however, legislative compromises were struck in the early years of the Tesla wars to limit direct sales to Tesla. In 2014, the car dealers successfully lobbied the New York legislature to ban direct sales, but the law grandfathered in Tesla's five existing locations in the state.[18] Rivian's Jim Chen, who happens to be a Buffalo native, fumed at the unfairness of forcing Buffalo residents to travel out of state to test drive a Rivian.[19] He could have added that it's grossly unfair that Tesla gets some dealerships in the state, whereas its chief rival is frozen out.

A similar law is still on the books in Washington state. In 2014, the legislature passed a statute generally prohibiting direct sales but providing that

> [a] manufacturer that held a vehicle dealer license in this state on January 1, 2014, to own, operate, or control a new motor vehicle dealership that sells new vehicles that are only of that manufacturer's makes or lines and that are not sold new by a licensed independent franchise dealer, or to own, operate, or control or contract with companies that provide finance, leasing, or service for vehicles that are of that manufacturer's makes or lines.[20]

That exemption covers only Tesla, leaving Rivian, Lucid, and other EV start-ups out of luck in the Evergreen State. As GeekWire reported in 2024, for now, Rivian has a "space" at Seattle's University Village shopping center and Lucid has a "studio" at the upscale outdoor mall. Shoppers can get inside parked cars and learn about the vehicles. But unlike a Tesla showroom – including one that's located at the same mall – Rivian and Lucid cannot give shoppers a test drive, sell them a car, or discuss financing for purchases.

Needless to say, this sort of handcuffing puts Tesla's rivals at a serious competitive disadvantage. Paula Sardinas is the CEO and President of Washington Build Back Black Alliance, which supports expanded direct sales. She quipped "In God we trust – everybody else I've got to test drive."[21] Despite persistent lobbying efforts to change the law by the EV start-ups and their environmentalist allies, Washington's dealers have thus far prevented the issue from being revisited in the legislature.

As of this writing, the Electrification Coalition counts nine states in which Tesla has some sort of legislative carve-out, but other EV start-ups are shut out from direct sales.[22] Although, as discussed further in Chapter 9, exact number counts are complicated because of changing state laws and interpretive questions, this list would include at least Pennsylvania, Mississippi, Ohio, Maryland, and North Carolina.

Special carve-outs for Tesla raise serious questions not only of fairness but also of constitutionality. The Fourteenth Amendment to the United States Constitution guarantees "the equal protection of the laws." Further, many state constitutions contain provisions that require that laws be "general" and not "special," meaning that laws must apply to all similarly situated individuals or companies.[23] These laws were intended to prevent the practice of companies finding friends in the legislature to grant them special privileges like chartering banks or building railroads – in other words, to stop crony capitalism. State courts have applied these principles to invalidate just the sort of special exemptions from general laws we see in some of the Tesla carve-outs. A 1981 decision of the Maryland Court of Appeals[24] demonstrates the application of this principle in a circumstance that hits close to home. Maryland law generally prohibited producers or refiners of petroleum products from operating retail gasoline service stations with their own personnel or with a subsidiary company, but the legislature made a special exception that "in practical effect allow[ed] only one producer and refiner of petroleum products (the Mobil Corporation) to continue operating retail gasoline service stations through one of its wholly owned subsidiaries (Montgomery Ward & Co., Inc.)." The court held that the legislature couldn't prohibit direct sales of gasoline for everyone, but make a special carve-out for Mobil. It's not hard to see how this principle could be applied to direct sales of cars.

The coalition supporting direct sales has hesitated to go down this road because there's a complicated question of remedy once the unconstitutionality of special carve-outs is established. Would a court say that Rivian and Lucid can do it too, or that Tesla can't do it anymore? The last thing that I would want is to push a legal argument that has the effect of *retracting* direct sales. My own view is that the better approach as a matter of law would be to hold that any company similarly situated to Tesla – that is, an EV-only manufacturer – should be allowed the same privileges as Tesla. Trying to take back Tesla's privileges after the company has made substantial investments in reliance on the legislative carveout would raise its own constitutional questions. Nonetheless, there is some legal risk to the continuing viability of direct sales in pushing this argument.

If the legal argument is complicated, the policy argument is a no-brainer. It is simply indefensible that one company should be allowed to sell to its own customers while other companies that are in the exact same situation – EV manufacturers that don't use franchised dealers – cannot. This is particularly true given the immense competitive imbalance such a scheme creates. As we've seen throughout this book, the EV start-ups contend that franchised dealer sales are not viable for them. That leaves them in the Washington situation – opening small galleries to showcase their cars without being able to give test drives, take trade-ins, talk prices or financing, or any of the other key aspects of selling cars. Meanwhile, Tesla can operate with full freedom, at least at the locations it's permitted by state law.

To be clear, none of this is Tesla's fault. It did not ask for carve-outs limited to itself, nor has it opposed efforts to allow direct sales for others. The company has repeatedly assured me that it supports direct sales for all. I wish that the company would make that case publicly and loudly, but maybe that's too much to expect from a company whose mission is to make money, not to save the world. Further, Tesla deserves immense credit for paving the way for the EV start-ups that followed. As we'll see in Chapter 9, it's opened the doors to its followers in many more states than it's closed them. And even in the states where the others are shut out for the present, the Tesla carve-outs have paved the way for the others to follow eventually. Special privileges for Tesla alone are unsustainable. The camel has its nose in the tent, and the rest of its body will follow.

Notes

1. Carmine Gallo, "Rivian Founder RJ Scaringe Uses Storytelling to Power His IPO Presentation," Forbes, April 21, 2022, www.forbes.com/sites/carminegallo/2021/11/10/rivian-founder-rj-scaringe-uses-storytelling-to-power-his-ipo-presentation/?sh=39c1b0ee6a7d.
2. Ibid.
3. "Say Hello to Elio. The Ultra-High-Mileage, Sleek Two-Seater for an Incredibly Affordable Base Price. Coming Fourth Quarter 2016!," Elio Motors, www.eliomotors.com (last visited November 14, 2015).
4. "Are Dealerships Available to Purchase?," Elio Motors, https://eliomotors.zendesk.com/hc/en-us/articles/203014734-Are-dealerships-available-to-purchase-.
5. Transcript, "Auto Distribution: Current Issues and Future Trends," Workshop Hosted by the Federal Trade Commission, January 19, 2016, www.ftc.gov/system/files/documents/public_events/895193/auto_distribution_transcript.pdf.
6. Dan Neil, "Rivian's Delivery Van: Not Just for Bezos Anymore," The Wall Street Journal, March 21, 2024, www.wsj.com/lifestyle/cars/rivians-delivery-van-not-just-for-bezos-anymore-038f0260.
7. "Statement of Rivian Automotive, LLC on Nevada AB 114 regarding Direct Sales Position: Proponent," March 2, 2021, www.leg.state.nv.us/App/NELIS/REL/81st2021/ExhibitDocument/OpenExhibitDocument?exhibitId=47814&fileDownloadName=0302_AB114_Rivian.Automotive_sptltr.pdf.
8. Ibid.
9. Ibid.
10. Ibid.
11. Brandon L. Bigelow, "Virginia and West Virginia Adopt Laws Regulating Over-the-Air Updates, Seyfarth Legal Update," June 24, 2022, www.seyfarth.com/news-insights/virginia-and-west-virginia-adopt-laws-regulating-over-the-air-updates.html.
12. "Plan your next visit," Rivian, https://rivian.com/spaces/locations.
13. Sean Tucker, "Consumer Reports: Rivian Owners Most Satisfied Drivers," Kelley Blue Book, February 6, 2024, www.kbb.com/car-news/consumer-reports-rivian-owners-most-satisfied-drivers/.

14. "Giving Fleets the Freedom to Buy," Electrification Coalition, October 25, 2022, https://electrificationcoalition.org/resource/giving-fleets-the-freedom-to-buy/.
15. Scooter Doll, "Lucid Shares EPA Range for Air Models Including 520 Miles on the Dream Edition Range," Electrek, September 16, 2021, https://electrek.co/2021/09/16/lucid-shares-epa-range-for-air-models-including-520-miles-on-the-dream-edition-range/.
16. *Lucid Group, U.S.A., Inc. v. Johnston*, 2023 WL 5688153, No. 22-CV-1116-RP (W.D. Tex. June 21, 2023).
17. Nikola Corporation, Form S-1, Registration Statement under the Securities Act of 1933, www.sec.gov/Archives/edgar/data/1731289/000104746920004147/a2241967zs-1.htm#da48601_risk_factors.
18. Chris Bragg, "Inside New York State's Fight Over How EVs Are Sold," GovTech, December 13, 2022, www.govtech.com/transportation/inside-new-york-states-fight-over-how-evs-are-sold.
19. Ibid.
20. Wash. Rev. Code § 46.96.185(1)(g)(vii) (2018).
21. Ibid.
22. "Freedom to Buy Vehicles in Pennsylvania," Electrification Coalition, https://electrificationcoalition.org/work/state-ev-policy/pennsylvania-ev-policy/freedom-to-buy-vehicles-in-pennsylvania/ (last visited February 15, 2025).
23. Naomi R. Lamoreaux & John Joseph Wallis, "Economic Cris, General Laws, and the Mid-Nineteenth-Century Transformation of American Political Economy" (2021) *Journal of the Early Republic* 403–33.
24. *4 Cities Service Co. v. Governor, State of Maryland*, 431 A 2d 663 (Md. Ct. App. 1981).

9 HOW TESLA TURNED THE TIDE

It's fair to say that Todd Maron has a complicated relationship with Elon Musk. The New York University trained lawyer was practicing family law in California when he landed Musk as a client in Musk's divorces from Justine Wilson and Talulah Riley (whom he remarried and then divorced for a second time). Musk was so impressed with Maron that, in 2013, he hired him as Tesla's General Counsel. There's a big difference between representing clients in divorces and running the legal department of a fast-growing company like Tesla, but Maron met the task with aplomb. In a company with a high turnover right among top executives, including general counsels, Maron demonstrated what passes for great longevity, departing the company in 2018. Along the way, he helped both Tesla and Musk navigate many rocky shoals, including more family troubles, fatal crashes, complaints about workplace conditions, and shareholder lawsuits. And, of course, Tesla's wars with the car dealers.

In 2024, after he had been away from Tesla for six years, Maron again made news in Musk's orbit when he testified in a Delaware shareholder lawsuit over a $56 billion compensation package approved for Musk during Maron's tenure. Judge Kathaleen McCormick struck the pay package, finding that it had not been fair to shareholders and that the Tesla executives who approved it had not been at arm's length from Musk. Among other things, Judge McCormick cited Maron's deposition in the case, finding that his "admiration for Musk moved him to tears during his deposition."[1] Todd Maron, a rock for Musk during his divorce proceedings and five tumultuous years as his General Counsel, remained personally and emotionally loyal to his boss even after the strain of working hand-in-hand with one of the world's most demanding and complex figures.

The Tesla wars have been anything but conventional because the man at the top is anything but conventional. During his crucial years at the company, Maron had to navigate not only the complicated legal and political world of the car dealers and their legacy supporters but also his boss's often shifting and unpredictable decisions and strategies. The same is true for everyone else at the company. So how did it all work out?

The title of this book asserts that Tesla smashed the car dealers' monopoly. Some might say that's an exaggeration and that battles over direct sales are still ongoing. They certainly are. As of this writing, Tesla is still blocked from selling direct in some states, is continuing to litigate its right to sell in other states, and is locked with the car dealers in high-stakes litigation in Louisiana. Bills that would either help or hurt Tesla continue to be introduced in legislatures. Skirmishing over direct sales may continue for quite some time.

But, whatever twists and turns lie ahead in courts, motor vehicle commissions, legislatures, and governors' offices, Tesla has already smashed the car dealers' monopoly. The legal, political, and business strategies adopted by Todd Maron and others at Tesla have worked. Over the last decade, Tesla has sold over two million cars across the United States, none of them through a dealer. It has opened sales centers in thirty-six states (and the District of Columbia) and service centers in thirty-four states.[2] Even if some of those sales centers are technically "galleries" where customers can't take a test drive, trade in a car, or get a price quote, Tesla has found a way to disintermediate the dealers while reaching the vast majority of Americans who want to buy its cars.

And it's not going back. The dealers' arguments hinged on direct sales representing a threat to consumer interests. In the early days of the direct sales wars, those arguments were theoretical and had to be given mostly theoretical responses (as we saw in Chapter 3). But now consumers have a decade of experience with Tesla direct sales. The dealers' predictions that the sky would fall in on consumers have not happened. To the contrary, the majority of Tesla customers love the company and the way it does business. Although Rivian knocked

Tesla off the top perch for customer satisfaction in 2024 (as we saw in Chapter 8), Tesla buyers are an extraordinarily loyal bunch. According to a 2023 article by Customergauge, Tesla's "customers are committed, passionate, and happy to spread the word."[3] A Bloomberg study found that 99% of Tesla Model 3 customers would recommend the car to friends or family.[4] An Experian study found that 74.7% of customers who disposed of a Tesla bought a new one.[5] Tesla's net promoter score – the answer to the question of how likely a customer is to recommend a company – is an astonishingly high 97, one of the highest of any brand in the world.[6] Tesla customers have experience buying direct from Tesla and having the company service their cars.

Disappointingly for the dealers, there is not a shred of sentiment among Tesla customers for requiring Tesla to sell through dealers. And, whereas in the early years Tesla had to make its own case for direct sales, now it has two million loyal customers making its case too. When Tesla has to argue its case in administrative hearings or legislatures, it is now often joined by Tesla owners from that state eager to give their officials an earful about letting them buy as they please. I wouldn't want the dealers' job of explaining why the voters sitting across the table shouldn't be allowed to buy a legal product from a car company they love.

There's no going back. As we saw in Chapter 3, incumbency is a big advantage. When Tesla was trying to break in around 2014, the car dealers were the incumbents. They could rely on the laws that had protected them against competition for many decades. But, after a decade of success with direct sales, Tesla's becoming somewhat of an incumbent itself. It's invested in many states, hired people, paid taxes, and developed a broad customer base. For any significant state to rip away Tesla's right to sell direct feels like a hill too high. Increasingly, direct sales is a one-way ratchet. The states that permit it can't take it back. The states that limit it can only allow it more. And the states that ban it are becoming increasingly isolated and under legal and political pressure to change. While many battles remain to be fought, it is doubtful that, in another ten years' time, many states, if any, will continue to prohibit direct sales.

Getting to this place wasn't easy. Not only did the dealers have the incumbency position in many states, and not only are the politics complicated for the reasons reviewed in Chapter 7, but Tesla didn't always make the job easy on itself. A high rate of turnover in top executives has complicated the company's efforts to maintain a consistent public interface and strategy on the direct sales issues. For example, between Maron's departure in 2018 and 2023, Tesla had four different general counsels,[7] which created serious issues with respect to maintaining a consistent legal and political strategy. In other areas of the company, there was often a "left hand doesn't know what the right hand's doing" phenomenon that tended to undermine the company's public efforts.

I experienced this firsthand in 2019 while working with one of Tesla's regional government relations teams on a push for legislation permitting direct sales in Connecticut. I gave testimony to the Connecticut legislature and was preparing an op-ed. In the midst of these efforts, Elon Musk made the dumbfounding announcement that Tesla would close most of its bricks-and-mortar stores and move its sales online.[8] The entire premise of the direct sales position was that Tesla and other electric vehicle (EV) start-ups needed a bricks-and-mortar presence in order to sell and service their cars (even states that prohibited direct sales couldn't stop Tesla from selling online). If Tesla was going all online, there was no need for our efforts. Tesla's employees could just sneak away, but I was going to look like an idiot. I reached out to my Tesla contacts on the Connecticut push and asked what was going on. They were as dumbfounded as I was. A week or two later, Tesla reversed course, and things were back to business on direct sales. I was relieved but a little nervous going forward.

Notwithstanding all of the challenges of launching a new company with a revolutionary product while fighting legal, regulatory, and political battles against a highly resourced set of incumbents, Tesla and its allies turned the tide. The map of where Tesla can sell direct today is far greener than red. Reporters often ask me for a list of where direct sales are permitted and prohibited, and I have to say that it's not quite as binary as that. While the situation is clear in some states, it's more complicated in others. For example, many reporters list Michigan as a "closed" state, but (as discussed in Chapter 6), the 2020 settlement in Michigan effectively gives Tesla the right to run nearly complete retail stores and service centers even though it nominally still can't "sell" in Michigan. In other states, Tesla and other EV manufacturers have to get special permission from the motor vehicle commission to open a store in a particular location. In yet other states, litigation over exactly what the franchise dealer law means and how it applies to Tesla or other companies remains ongoing. Finally, because the situation in some states remains fluid, any open/closed list may be outdated shortly after it's written.

All that said, readers of this book will want to know where things stand as of this writing, so I've grouped the states into various clusters. Here goes.

ALWAYS OPEN

California's franchise dealer law protects dealers from manufacturer competition by only prohibiting a manufacturer "[t]o compete with a dealer in the same line-make operating under an agreement or franchise from a manufacturer or distributor in the relevant market area," which is defined as a 10-mile radius from dealer location.[9] Since the EV start-ups don't have franchised dealers at all, they can open dealerships in California as they please. At times, some of the dealers have grumbled that maybe California law does block direct sales, but in a 2017 submission to the Federal Trade Commission, the California New Car Dealers Association admitted that "California does not prohibit direct sales of vehicles by manufacturers." It's not hard to see why the dealers would like to find a way for California law to block direct sales. A report in *Automotive News* found that Tesla's direct sales cost California dealers a total of $910 or $700,000 per dealer in 2022.[10]

Tesla did not have to fight the direct sales wars in its home turf in California because the state was already open. Since California accounts for about a fifth of national GDP, getting a foothold in California is already a big step toward establishing the success of the direct sales model. And California also tends to be a thought leader. If other states are serious about wanting to honor the motivations behind the original franchise dealer laws – protecting dealers from competition by their own franchising manufacturers – then the California law is a model of how to do that without stifling direct sales by manufacturers that don't franchise at all, or even by manufacturers that do franchise but want to open stores in locations where they don't have franchisees.

NEW LEGISLATION ALLOWS DIRECT SALES

As we saw in Chapter 5, Colorado passed legislation allowing direct sales by EV-only manufacturers in 2020. The Colorado legislature has not been alone in responding to the new technological and business realities by updating its laws to permit EV direct sales. New Hampshire may have been the first to move, passing legislation in 2013 allowing car makers with no franchised dealers to open their own stores.[11] Utah passed a similar law allowing direct sales in 2018.[12] Vermont legislation allowed for direct sales of EVs in 2021.[13] Different states have their own unique motivations for allowing direct sales. Wyoming, where coal production is a major part of the economy, passed a law permitting direct sales in 2017 in the hopes that it would boost demand for coal.[14]

In Florida, Governor Ron DeSantis signed legislation in 2023 that bans direct sales but contains an exception for manufacturers without franchisees.[15] The Alliance for Automotive Innovation, which represents legacies like Ford and Stellantis, urged DeSantis to veto the legislation, arguing that it would "make buying a vehicle more cumbersome" and would "make vehicles more expensive to own by continuing to add unnecessary costs to the motor vehicle franchise system," but once again, the legacies saw their chance to play on a level playing field with the EV start-ups slipping away.

NEW LEGISLATION ALLOWS LIMITED DIRECT SALES OR GRANDFATHERING

Many states have taken a grudging approach to direct sales, either grandfathering in Tesla's existing stores or allowing direct sales by EV-only manufactures subject to a cap. As we saw in Chapter 8, New

York grandfathered in Tesla's five existing stores but said no to more stores or other manufacturers, and Washington also carved out a special exception for Tesla. Indiana also banned direct sales for everyone but grandfathered in Tesla.[16] The New Jersey and Ohio laws, discussed in Chapter 3, allow EV-only manufacturers to open up to four stores in New Jersey and just Tesla to open up to three stores in Ohio. A 2014 Pennsylvania law allowed Tesla – but only Tesla – to open up to five stores.[17] Georgia similarly passed a law permitting direct sales by only Tesla.[18] Maryland similarly allowed up to four EV-only manufacturers to open up to four stores.[19] In 2017, North Carolina adopted a law permitting direct sales by EV-only manufacturers, but with a six-store limit.[20] In the negotiations over the opening of its Gigafactory in Nevada, Tesla was able to secure an exception from the state's direct sales ban for just itself.[21]

In 2023, Mississippi banned direct sales but grandfathered in Tesla's existing store in Brandon.[22] Republican Governor Tate Reeves defied Republican calls to veto the bill, saying that "[a]lmost 200 small businesses in communities across our state are seeking assurances that big manufacturers can't just destroy their businesses."[23] Someone should do an audit on exactly how "small" those businesses are. According to NADA data, the average Mississippi dealership had over $48 million in revenue in 2023,[24] which does not even account for the fact that many dealerships are part of wider ownership groups. Nonetheless, the "mom and pop" politics of the mid-1950s prevailed again in Mississippi. Like Governor Snyder in Michigan (see Chapter 6), Governor Reeves also promised to revisit the issue, acknowledging that "with new innovation comes new companies with new business models."[25] Good luck, Mississippi. Mississippi should really be in *Closed* category (later), but since the law grandfathers in one Tesla store, it stays in this bucket.

LITIGATION OR ADMINISTRATIVE PROCESS SECURES RIGHT TO DIRECT SALES

Some of Tesla's most dramatic victories in the direct sales wars have landed through litigation. In earlier chapters, we saw how Tesla beat the car dealers in court in Massachusetts and how it obtained a favorable settlement through constitutional litigation in Michigan. In Illinois, Tesla entered into another favorable settlement, this time with the Secretary of State, which allows Tesla to open up to thirteen stores.[26] When the Secretary of State negotiated similar deals for Rivian and Lucid, the Illinois Automobile Dealers Association sued to block them. The trial court dismissed the dealers' complaint, finding that Illinois law does not prohibit manufacturers from becoming dealers.[27] In Missouri, then Attorney General (now Senator) Josh Hawley successfully defended the Missouri Department of Revenue in a dealer challenge to the state's issuance of a dealer license to Tesla.[28] Like other courts that have considered legal challenges by dealers, the Missouri court found that the dealers lacked standing to sue.

One of my favorite stories of Tesla's litigation success came in 2023 in Delaware. When Tesla applied for a dealer's license, the Division of Motor Vehicles held a hearing before an administrative law judge to determine if Tesla was qualified to hold a license under Delaware law. As I often do, I testified for Tesla at the hearing, making the usual case that the original purpose of the direct sales prohibitions was to protect dealers in existing franchise relationships with manufacturers, not to prohibit pure direct sales, and that allowing EV start-ups to sell direct was in the interest of consumers. A lawyer for the state cross-examined me, apparently certain that, despite my sworn statement that I was not being, and never had been, paid by Tesla, there must be some secret source of funding. What else could explain a law professor's willingness to take the position that had been backed by ... let's see, the environmentalists, the consumer protection groups, the free market groups, the FTC, and every other public interest or academic group that had weighed in? Tesla lost at the hearing, and then again in the trial court, but in 2023 won a landmark case in the Delaware Supreme Court.[29] The court ruled that the Delaware statute's "definitions exclude Tesla and its direct sales model, where new electric cars are not sold through franchised dealers in Delaware."[30]

Despite the Delaware example, Tesla has generally fared well in administrative proceedings. In Minnesota, the Department of Public Safety ruled that Minnesota's franchise dealer laws "does not prohibit a [car] manufacturer from becoming licensed as a dealer in

Minnesota."[31] The dealers tried to get the legislature to change this and prohibit direct sales, but (once again showing the importance of playing defense rather than offense), the effort failed. In Rhode Island, the Motor Vehicle Dealers' License and Hearing Board, apparently influenced by the 2014 Supreme Judicial Court decision in neighboring Massachusetts, issued a ruling that state law did not prohibit direct sales by manufacturers that don't use dealers.[32] An Arizona administrative law judge reached the same conclusion in 2017, holding that the Arizona Department of Transportation had incorrectly interpreted the state's law as prohibiting direct sales by manufacturers that use a pure direct sales model.[33] Despite their proximity to the dealers, the bureaucrats have usually been on Tesla's side on the interpretation of the laws.

DIRECT SALES PERMITTED WITH ADMINISTRATIVE APPROVAL

Several states have direct sales laws that don't categorically prohibit direct sales but require a manufacturer seeking to open its own stores to obtain permission from the administrative agency that handles car dealer licensing, typically called something like the division of motor vehicles. For example, the Virginia Motor Vehicle Code provides that

> [t]he ownership, operation, or control of a dealership by a manufacturer, factory branch, distributor, distributor branch, or subsidiary thereof [is allowed] if the Commissioner [of motor vehicles] determines, after a hearing at the request of any party, that there is no dealer independent of the manufacturer or distributor, factory branch or distributor branch, or subsidiary thereof available in the community or trade area to own and operate the franchise in a manner consistent with the public interest.[34]

Kentucky and Wisconsin have similar statutes. To get approval to open a store in these states, Tesla or other EV start-ups have to file a petition with the Department of Motor Vehicles and then demonstrate, at a public hearing, that there isn't a dealer available to open a dealership on behalf of the company and that allowing a company-owned store in a particular location would be in the public interest.

I've testified for Tesla, Rivian, and Lucid in such hearings, and they're always interesting. The easy part, at least for me, is making the case that the public interest supports allowing car companies to open their own stores. Tesla owners frequently show up at these hearings to make the case even better than I can. To them, this isn't academic, it's personal. It's also straightforward to present the case that the dealers wouldn't do a good job of selling Teslas, Rivians, or Lucids, for the many reasons discussed throughout this book (particularly in Chapter 2). Nonetheless, the dealers' lawyers sometimes try to muddy these waters by getting particular dealers to make a proffer that they would be interested in becoming a Tesla franchisee. I'm not sure about the sincerity of these proffers, but thus far they haven't been particularly effective. In a 2016 decision in Virginia, the administrative law judge found that the five dealers that testified they were interested in a Tesla dealership "admitted that they had not performed any economic analysis to establish whether or not a Tesla dealership would be financially possible."[35] When "the owner of several dealerships in Newport News and Richmond, was asked if would be willing to make property available for a Tesla dealership, he stated, 'possibly.'" Hardly a rousing statement of readiness for the task!

To date, the EV start-ups have won their hearings in Virginia and Kentucky and we're waiting on Wisconsin. It will be particularly interesting to see how things go in the Badger State. As discussed in Chapter 1, it was Wisconsin that kicked off the state dealer franchise laws in the 1930s. Wisconsin was a thought leader then, and it has another chance to be a thought leader now.

CLOSED

That brings us to the states that continue to categorically ban direct sales: Alabama, Arkansas, Connecticut, Iowa, Kansas, Louisiana, Montana, Nebraska, New Mexico, North Dakota, Oklahoma, South Carolina, South Dakota, Texas, and West Virginia. Some, like Kansas, have such a broad definition of "sales" that even display galleries are prohibited. Others, like Texas, allow galleries, while holding the line at full sales transactions. Some ban sales by manufacturers, but are less clear about service. Even if Tesla can't open its own stores to sell cars in a state, it's critical that it be able to provide warranty repairs and other service for its vehicles.

Most of the states that ban direct sales do so based on adhering to their original direct sales prohibitions rather than on new bans in response to Tesla's entry, but some have passed new legislation specifically to block Tesla. West Virginia passed an anti-Tesla bill in 2015,[36] and, in 2021, Arkansas closed an apparent loophole that would have allowed Tesla to lease rather than sell cars. On the other hand, bills that would allow some form of direct sales by EV manufacturers have been introduced in many of these states, over the fierce objection of the car dealers' lobby. For example, there has been hope of a direct sales breakthrough in Connecticut for a number of legislative sessions running. But, as noted in Chapter 7, the politics of direct sales are complicated.

On the other hand, as discussed in greater detail in Chapter 8, there are ongoing lawsuits by Tesla and Lucid that could shake up the recalcitrant states. If Lucid wins its constitutional challenge in Texas, the door could quickly open for direct sales across much of the remaining holdout territory. Tesla's challenge in Louisiana is more focused, but it received a boost when the Biden Administration's Justice Department weighed in with an *amicus curiae* (friend of the court) brief supporting Tesla's argument that the district court erred in dismissing its antitrust claims.[37] The federal court of appeals for the Fifth Circuit handed Tesla a significant victory in August 2024, rejecting one of Tesla's constitutional challenges (equal protection) but allowing another constitutional challenge (due process) and an antitrust theory to proceed.[38] Regardless of the outcome of these cases, the closed states are feeling the heat from litigation, lobbying, and, most importantly, voters who also happen to be consumers and are increasingly fed up that they don't have the opportunity to buy a Tesla or other EV or have it serviced in the same ways that are available to the citizens of most other states.

TRIBAL LANDS

Perhaps my very favorite twist in the direct sales wars concerns the role of Native American tribes in fixing the problem for the rest of us.

For many years, tribal lands have been the place for activities that state law prohibited – particularly casinos. As the direct sales wars heated up and Tesla faced the brick wall erected by the car dealers in some states, it had the brilliant idea of asking some of the tribes whether they might be interested in making money by leasing Tesla some real estate. A sales and service center for cars comes with none of the seediness or possible negative spillover effects of a casino, so it was a natural economic opportunity for the tribes. In 2021, Tesla opened its first store on tribal lands – on the lands of the Nambé Pueblo, north of Santa Fe, New Mexico. Later the same year, it opened a second showroom in New Mexico on the lands of the Santa Ana Pueblo. Tesla then went on to partner with the Mohegan tribe in Connecticut and is working with the Oneida nation in upstate New York.

The car dealers have been seething at Tesla's clever strategy. Jeff Aiosa, executive director of the Connecticut auto dealers association, fumed that "[i]t's not fair to have an unlevel playing field when all the other manufacturers abide by the state franchise laws and Tesla wants this exception to go around the law. I would suggest their pivoting to the sovereign nation is representative of them not wanting to abide by the law."[39] Sorry, Mr. Aiosa, but Tesla is playing by the law exactly. Native tribes have the sovereignty to make their own decisions on these things, and it's just as lawful for them to permit direct sales on their land as it is for Connecticut's neighbors in Massachusetts and Rhode Island. As to an "unlevel playing field" with the other manufacturers, I couldn't agree more, which is why the legacies should be allowed to sell direct too. Surely you meant that the right response to one company finding a way to distribute its products more efficiently is to allow everyone else to do it too!

Tesla's tribal land strategy should leave the dealers worried about continuing to block direct sales in the holdout states. Thirty-nine states have at least one tribal nation with the rights to manage its own land, so there is plenty of room to grow. While it may not be ideal for Tesla or the other EV start-ups to have to fill in all of their gaps by opening stores on tribal lands, it's a second-best solution that can work in many places. In combination with the fact that Tesla can already sell and service its cars in the majority of states, the tribal land strategy may put the nail in the coffin of the dealers' last stand against direct sales.

The alert reader may notice that I have not accounted in this chapter for Alaska, Hawaii, Idaho, Maine, Oregon, or Tennessee. In those states, the application of the state's dealer franchise laws to direct sales is unclear and, to my knowledge, has not yet been tested.[40] Over time, it likely will be. There is plenty more work to do on the direct sales front. The war may be drawing to a close, but there are battles still to fight.

I may be hasty in calling the direct sales wars in Tesla's favor, but there's considerable evidence that Tesla is now in "mopping up" mode. Between open states, half-open states, and native lands, Tesla has established a footprint across much of the country. It is unlikely that states that now permit Tesla will go back, and quite likely that the holdout states will go forward, either through political processes or because a court tells them they have to. Against the backdrop of these political, regulatory, and legal battles, Tesla has established a loyal base of customers, proved that direct sales can work, and defeated the manufacturers' predictions that the sky will fall on consumers if a car company can sell and service its own product. The dealers started out as incumbents, but they're increasingly having to play offense and make the case for taking away a successful business model that consumers seem to like. Given the pan-ideological set of interest groups supporting the direct sales cause, the splintering of opinion in both political parties, and the inherent power of the status quo, that seems a high hurdle for the dealers to jump.

While I'm calling Tesla's war for Tesla, I'm far from prepared to call the direct sales issue resolved in general. Many states still exclude direct sales by other EV start-ups, and most of them exclude direct sales by the legacies. That creates an uneven playing field that needs urgent attention. Further, the advent of EVs is hardly the only technological revolution shaking up the automobile industry. The advent of connected and automated vehicles and artificial intelligence promises to revolutionize the way people buy cars, share cars, and access transportation services in ways that make the EV revolution seem mild. In Chapter 10, we will consider the road ahead, both in terms of potential solutions to the direct sales issue and how coming technological waves may dramatically shift the discussion.

Notes

1. Thomas Germain, "A former Tesla Lawyer Broke Down in Tears during Elon Musk's Compensation Lawsuit," Quartz, February 1, 2024, https://qz.com/elon-musk-tesla-pay-lawsuit-todd-maron-1851217016.
2. "US Tesla Stores and Galleries," Tesla, www.tesla.com/findus/list/stores/United%20States.
3. Sabrina Tessitore, "Tesla's NPS Score: What's Driving Tesla's Customer Loyalty?," CustomerGauge https://customergauge.com/benchmarks/blog/tesla-nps-score (last visited February 16, 2025).
4. Ibid.
5. Ibid.
6. Ibid.
7. Fred Lambert, "Tesla Hires New General Counsel – A Position It Has a Hard Time Filling," Electrek, February 10, 2023, https://electrek.co/2023/02/10/tesla-hires-general-counsel-position-hard-time-to-fill/.
8. Lauren Thomas, "Tesla Reportedly Moving Out of Malls, Dealing Another Blow to Shopping Center Owners," CNBC, July 28, 2021, www.cnbc.com/2021/07/28/tesla-reportedly-moving-out-of-malls-a-blow-to-shopping-center-owners.html#:~:text=Tesla%20is%20shuttering%20a%20number,has%20wavered%20in%20recent%20years.
9. Cal. Veh. Code § 11713.3.
10. Hannah Lutz, "Tesla, Other EV Makers Likely Cost California Dealers $910 Million in 2022 Profit Opportunity," Automotive News, May 12, 2023, www.autonews.com/dealers/tesla-rivian-lucid-direct-ev-sales-likely-cost-california-dealers-910m.
11. N.H. Rev. Stat. Ann. §§ 357-C:1 – 357:-C:16.
12. Joshua Ellis, "Tesla Enters Utah Market as More Drivers Switch to Electric," The Daily Universe, April 19, 2018, https://universe.byu.edu/2018/04/19/tesla-enters-utah-market-as-more-drivers-switch-to-electric/.
13. Michelle Lewis, "The First Tesla Store Is Finally Open in EV-Loving Vermont," Electrek, March 6, 2024, https://electrek.co/2024/03/06/first-tesla-store-vermont/.
14. Laura Hancock, "Legislature Passes a Bill that Would Allow Tesla to Open," Casper Star-Tribune, March 2, 2017, https://trib.com/news/state-regional/govt-and-politics/legislature-passes-a-bill-that-would-allow-tesla-to-open/article_c35d1d64-3392-5bad-837a-adefbd3f7927.html.
15. www.winknews.com/making_ends_meet/florida-bans-direct-to-consumer-auto-sales-but-leaves-carve-out-for-tesla/article_c8aaf788-9e7e-5b0a-9a97-d5c8f2120a8f.html.
16. Fred Lambert, "Tesla Escapes Ban in Indiana by Being 'Grandfathered In', but the State Moves Forward with Ban on Direct Sales," Electrek, February 2, 2017, https://electrek.co/2017/02/02/tesla-indiana-grandfathered-in-ban/.

17. Nora Naughton, "Tesla Cleared to Open Up to 5 Stores in Pa. under New Law," Automotive News, July 11, 2014, www.autonews.com/article/20140711/RETAIL/140719962/tesla-cleared-to-open-up-to-5-stores-in-pa-under-new-law.
18. Lurah Lowery, "Georgia Bill that Would Allow EV Direct Sales Stalls in Senate," Repairer Driven News, March 24, 2022, www.repairerdrivennews.com/2022/03/24/georgia-bill-that-would-allow-ev-direct-sales-stalls-in-senate/.
19. Angelo Young, "Tesla Motors Inc (TSLA) Wins Approval for Direct Car Sales in Maryland, Starting October 1," International Business Times, May 12, 2015, www.ibtimes.com/tesla-motors-inc-tsla-wins-approval-direct-car-sales-maryland-starting-october-1-1918655.
20. "Tesla Sales Model Gets Relief in North Carolina in Surprise Late-Session Bill," Teslarati, June 21, 2017, www.teslarati.com/tesla-sales-model-gets-relief-north-carolina-surprise-late-session-bill/.
21. Bloomberg, "Tesla Nevada Factory Deal Allows Direct-to-Consumer Sales," Autoweek, September 12, 2014, www.autoweek.com/news/a1905511/tesla-nevada-factory-deal-allowss-direct-consumer-sales/.
22. Associated Press, "New Law Restricts Electric Car Stores in Mississippi," 6 News, March 15, 2023, www.wate.com/news/new-law-restricts-electric-car-stores-in-mississippi/.
23. Ibid.
24. "2023 Annual Financial Profile of America's Franchised New-Car Dealerships," NADA Data, www.nada.org/media/4695/download?inline.
25. Ibid.
26. Ryan Denham, "Car Dealers Sue Rivian, Secretary of State Over EV Sales," WGLT, March 26, 2021, www.wglt.org/business-and-economy/2021-03-26/car-dealers-sue-rivian-secretary-of-state-over-ev-sales.
27. Ryan Denham, "Judge Rules in Rivian's Favor in Lawsuit Over Direct Sales to Consumers," WGLT, January 5, 2023, www.wglt.org/local-news/2023-01-05/judge-rules-in-rivians-favor-in-lawsuit-over-direct-sales-to-consumers.
28. *State ex rel. Missouri Automobile Dealers Association* v. *Missouri Department of Revenue*, 541 SW 3d 585 (Mo. Ct. App. 2017).
29. *Tesla, Inc.* v. *Delaware Division of Motor Vehicles*, 297 A 3d 625 (Del. 2023).
30. Ibid. at 627.
31. Steve Alexander, "Minnesota Sales of Electric, Gas Cars Collide," Star Tribune, March 13, 2013, www.startribune.com/minnesota-sales-of-electric-gas-cars-collide/197706621/.
32. Patrick Anderson, "Paving the Way: Popular Electric Car Manufacturer Given License to Sell Direct in R.I.," The Providence Journal, June 10, 2018, www.providencejournal.com/story/news/politics/government/2018/01/10/electric-car-manufacturer-tesla-granted-licenses-to-sell-direct-in-ri/16339278007/.

33. Ryan Randazso, "Yes, You Can Buy a Tesla Electric Car at Its Scottsdale Store," AZ Central, June 22, 2017, www.azcentral.com/story/money/business/tech/2017/06/22/tesla-selling-electric-cars-scottsdale-store-arizona/416527001/.
34. Va. Code § 46.2-1572(4).
35. Hearing Decision, Commonwealth of Virginia, Department of Motor Vehicles, Formal Evidentiary Hearing: Tesla Motors, Inc., File No. 2016-001- Request for a Hearing Pursuant to Va. Code §§ 46.2-1572(4) and 46.2-1573 to be a Dealer (Nov. 30, 2016).
36. David Kravets, "West Virginia Is the Latest State to Ban Tesla Direct Sales," Ars Technica, April 4, 2015, https://arstechnica.com/cars/2015/04/west-virginia-is-the-latest-state-to-ban-tesla-direct-sales/.
37. Brief for the United States of America as Amicus Curiae in Support of Neither Party, *Tesla, Inc. v. Louisiana Automobile Dealers Association*, No. 22-cv-02982-SSV-DPC (5th Cir. October 19, 2023), www.justice.gov/d9/2023-10/417214.pdf.
38. *Tesla, Inc. v. Louisiana Auto. Dealers Ass'n*, 113 F.4th 511 (5th Cir. 2024).
39. "Tesla Is Opening More Showrooms on Tribal Lands to Avoid State Laws Barring Direct Sales," CBS News, July 29, 2023, www.cbsnews.com/sacramento/news/automaker-tesla-is-opening-more-showrooms-on-tribal-lands-to-avoid-state-laws-barring-direct-sales/.
40. Anyone wishing for more specific analysis of state laws on a state-by-state basis may wish to consult the following analysis by the National Conference of State Legislatures, www.wispolitics.com/wp-content/uploads/2021/08/State-Laws-on-Direct-Sales.pdf.

10 THE ROAD AHEAD

In 2016, Google's Waymo autonomous vehicle division released a video of what they branded as the first truly driverless ride on a public road.[1] The video featured Steve Mahan, the former CEO of the Santa Clara Valley Blind Center, taking a solo drive through Austin, Texas. To a backdrop of swelling music, Mr. Mahan, who is blind, testified that he had never been in Austin, but now he was driving in Austin. He observed that it was a "profound experience for me to be alone in a car," and spoke with optimism about the potential of driverless cars to give autonomy and freedom back to millions of people with disabilities, visual or otherwise. Even for this cynical and jaded law professor, it was a hopeful and inspiring video.

Mr. Mahan's narrative points to the tremendous changes that are coming to cars and transportation more generally. The electric vehicle (EV) revolution on which this book has centered is just one of the many technological, business, and social revolutions that are radically changing how cars are bought, owned, serviced, driven, shared, and used. Driverless cars, vehicle-to-vehicle, vehicle-to-infrastructure, and vehicle-to-everything communications, artificial intelligence, quantum computing, nanotechnology, and countless more technologies that we haven't heard about yet are on the horizon. The magnitude of these coming revolutions will swamp the picayune battles between car dealers and EV start-ups on which this book has focused.

And yet, as we look to the road ahead, it is likely that political, legal, and regulatory questions about car distribution will continue to play a role in the grand narrative of the American automobile, and of the role of the American car industry in the world. As we close this book, let's widen our lens and consider the direct sales battles in the context of car distribution around the globe, in the long history of the American romance with automobiles, and of the coming wave of technologies that may change everything that we know about getting around.

The United States is an anomaly in prohibiting direct sales. There are few similar regulations in the industrialized world. In Europe, for example, manufacturers can and do own their own affiliated retail outlets, without any causing a political crisis.[2] Chinese, Canadian, and Australian markets also "all allow for vehicles to be sold through a variety of sales channels, including through direct-to-consumer models and through franchise dealerships."[3] The direct sales story in the United States must be understood through a historical, economic, and cultural lens that centers on the particular facts of the American car industry in the mid twentieth century: the Big Three triopoly, the convergence on a franchised dealer model of distribution, the dealers' ability to put aside their business rivalry and mobilize politically, and a political culture aimed at redistributing economic power.

The direct sales story must also be understood through the wider lens of America's continuing romance with the personal automobile. America's car culture is unique in the world. Americans own more cars per capita than almost any other country. The automobile is not just a mode of transportation or a consumer product. It is a symbol of freedom, defiance, conformity, identity, status, politics, sexuality, and so much more. We make songs about cars and sit in them to watch movies. We eat, make love, and die in them. A few of us are born in them too. From cradle to grave, Americans get their kicks on Route 66.

It's no wonder that the direct sales wars have touched a nerve that goes beyond the economic interests of the dealers. Business school professors will tell you that Tesla is disrupting a means of distribution, but the rest of us understand that it's also disrupting a way of life. The dealers are not wrong when they say the car dealership is woven into the fabric of America's towns and cities. Americans are some of the most innovative people in the history of the planet, but, paradoxically, they're some of the most nostalgic and conservative too. People may not like dealers, but do they really want Uftring Ford or Green Chevy to disappear from the strip malls on the edge of Peoria?

The Road Ahead

As we close this book, let's give some thought to the future of America's dealerships and car distribution more generally. The last chapter made the case that Tesla has largely won the direct sales wars. Does that mean that the dealers are done? Not necessarily. In the short run, at least, it's far from clear that direct sales will put the dealers out of business. Chapter 9 reported a study on the losses that the dealers have incurred from having to compete with Tesla in California, but that may largely be just the effect of a new entrant into the market. If a popular new car brand had entered the market and sold through new franchised dealers, the existing dealers would have lost out too.

For its part, the Electrification Coalition argues that direct sales have not hurt dealers, they've just made dealers have to compete better. The Coalition explains that

> [d]irect sales do not exclusively benefit consumers and EV-only manufacturers. According to data from the National Automobile Dealers Association, franchise dealers perform better in states that are open to direct sales. In states that were open to at least one EV manufacturer, franchise dealerships saw their sales revenue increase 58% between 2012 and 2019. During the same period, states closed to direct sales only saw a 29% increase in sales revenue. Dealership employment saw a similar trend- with open states seeing a 21% increase in employment while closed states only had a 12% increase in employment. Contrary to what has been portrayed, franchise dealerships in direct sales states are benefitting from additional market competition, not seeing their business model undercut.[4]

There's no doubt that increased competition can help an industry to perform better. In his landmark decision in *United States* v. *Alcoa*,[5] Judge Learned Hand noted that the "possession of unchallenged economic power deadens initiative, discourages thrift and depresses energy," and "that immunity from competition is a narcotic, and rivalry is a stimulant, to industrial progress; that the spur of constant stress is necessary to counteract an inevitable disposition to let well enough alone." Dealer spokespeople like Jim Appleton may deny that the franchise laws make them immune from competition, but there's no question that Tesla's entry with a spanking new product and an upset-the-apple-cart means of distributing it has given the dealers quite a kick in the pants. While the kick may sting in the rear, it may also be good for the soul. As Judge Hand explained, "competitors, versed in the craft as no consumer can be, will be quick to detect opportunities for saving and new shifts in production, and be eager to profit by them." The dealers are having to adapt to EV direct sales by asking themselves hard questions about how they can provide value to manufacturers and consumers in a fast-changing world. After decades in which they were largely protected by law from having to ask those questions, this is a good thing not just for consumers, but also for the dealers themselves.

Even if they were allowed to engage in direct sales, the legacies would be unlikely to abandon their dealer networks altogether. For one, the legacies have contracts with dealers that would continue to apply even if state laws no longer prohibited net sales. Beyond legalities, the legacies have invested billions of dollars in their dealer networks, and replacing them with a new set of company-owned stores would be extremely expensive. Further, the legacies appear sincerely to believe that their dealers provide value (at least sometimes). NADA trumpets a 2024 statement from General Motors (GM)'s President of North America Marissa West that "I became a hard fast believer that dealers are a competitive advantage."[6] As we previously saw, Mary Barra purports to agree. To repeat a point frequently made throughout this book, I have no dog in that fight. There is no inconsistency in saying that investing in a strong dealer network could be GM's best strategy, while going direct to consumers could be Tesla's. There's no one-size-fits-all model for selling and servicing cars, which is why the fight is to *allow* direct sales, not require them.

That said, the current status quo of direct sales laws creates an uneven playing field in desperate need of correction. Even if GM and the other legacies do not want to replace their dealer networks entirely, they need more flexibility to adapt to new technologies, new economic circumstances, and new consumer expectations. For example, the legacies need a lot more flexibility to manage online sales, move from a haggling model to flat pricing, move toward build-to-order, provide over-the-air updates, educate consumers, and have an ongoing direct relationship with consumers who drive their cars. They might also need to open their own showrooms, galleries, or kiosks in nontraditional places such as malls or urban centers in order to compete more effectively with the EV start-ups. They also might need to take over some aspects of service that have traditionally been handled by dealers.

As we've seen throughout this book, the dealers have historically invoked law and political processes to resist even small shifts in the legacies' business model, such as Ford's efforts to sell used cars on its website (Chapter 1) or the manufacturers' current plans for over-the-air updates (Chapter 8). This is happening again as the legacies try to shift toward EVs. As we saw in Chapter 5, in 2022 Ford announced a shift toward a new business model for selling EVs, which it calls its Model e Program. In order to sell Ford EVs, a dealer has to make a number of investments like installing fast EV chargers, providing access to rapid inventory replenishment, and enhancing repair and maintenance facilities.[7] The dealers also have to agree to use the "Ford .com e-commerce platform for all EV transactions and engage in transparent, 'no-haggle' pricing."[8] Although 65 percent of Ford's dealers have signed up, many dealers have resisted. In six states – Arkansas, Florida, Illinois, New York, North Carolina, and South Dakota – dealers or dealer associations have filed lawsuits or administrative challenges asserting that Ford's Model e Program violates their contractual rights and state franchise dealer laws. Among other things, the dealers contend that the program "(i) constitutes an unlawful modification of dealers' franchises, (ii) imposes an unfair, inequitable, and unreasonably discriminatory system of allocation and distribution on dealers, (iii) unlawfully sets the retail price at which dealers may sell or lease EVs, and (iv) unreasonably requires dealers to make substantial changes to their dealership facilities."

Point (iii) should be particularly irksome to anyone who cares about consumer interests. As we saw in Chapter 4, the haggling model of car sales ranks high on the list of consumer complaints about the sales process. As Rosemary Shahan noted, it's not only unpleasant and leaves many consumers feeling like they've been swindled, but it creates significant racial and gender disparities. The EV start-ups have read customer sentiment and moved to flat, no-haggle pricing. For the legacies to be able to compete against the start-ups, they need to be able to offer a comparable consumer experience. By insisting on the continuation of the haggling model, the dealers are not only screwing the American consumer, they're also putting in jeopardy the legacies' ability to rival the start-ups for EV sales.

The dealers' ongoing battles against Ford's Model e program represent all that's wrong with the dealers' mindset. They not only want to resist a manufacturer's right to sell and service its own products, but they also want to keep in place a rigid set of 1950s rules even as to manufacturers that do use dealers. This creates the worst possible scenario for the legacies. They can't sell direct, which is already a significant competitive disadvantage as we saw GM admit in Chapter 5, and they can't even adapt within the franchise-dealer system to meet popular aspects of the start-ups' business model. The dealers aren't trying to protect the franchise distribution model. They're trying to kill it.

Even if the legacies are not allowed to sell EVs to the public themselves, they must be allowed greater flexibility to compete with the EV start-ups. The dealers are no longer mom-and-pops that need protection from the manufacturers, and they should not be able to rely on decades-old laws that arose in very different circumstances than today. At a minimum, courts and legislatures need to take a hard look at the big picture of the American car industry in the twenty-first century and make sure that the legacies are not arbitrarily handcuffed in their ability to sell EVs.

And then there are the other EV start-ups like RJ Scaringe's Rivian and Lucid that find themselves frozen out in a number of states by laws that (unconstitutionally) make a special exception for Tesla (Chapter 8). If the case for giving the legacies more flexibility is strong, the case for allowing other EV start-ups the same rights as Tesla is unassailable. I'd wager a pretty penny that this imbalance will disappear before long. Particularly with the peculiar politics of Elon Musk and Donald Trump continuing to develop in weird and wonderful ways, it seems hard to imagine that blue or purple states like New York, Pennsylvania, Washington, Nevada, and Georgia are going to continue to allow Tesla to do as it pleases while shutting out other American EV start-ups with no political baggage. All the same, one shouldn't count on things to take care of themselves spontaneously. How can the imbalances be corrected?

One factor that could have a significant effect on the future of the direct sales issue is public interest in buying EVs. As we've seen throughout this book, the Tesla wars are in part a clash between Tesla and the car dealers, and in part chunks of a bigger conflict between EVs and internal combustion cars. From about 2014 to 2023, EV sales seemed to be making significant year-by-year gains, leaping from under 100,000 in 2014 to over 1.2 million in 2023.[9] In 2024, EV sales seemed to hit the skids. Goldman Sachs suggests that three factors may be behind the EV slowdown – lower prices for used EVs are making buyers reluctant about buying new ones, governmental policies favoring EVs are in doubt, and concerns about driving range and supercharger access are increasing.[10] If EV momentum slows, could that have a significant effect on the direct sales wars?

Although we're still in the middle of things, the most likely effect is that the direct sales wars will broaden away from Tesla. Up until recently, to the average consumer, EV was almost synonymous with Tesla. With Elon Musk increasingly entering the culture wars and bare-fisted MAGA politics, Tesla's brand is undergoing a social makeover. California was once Tesla's stronghold – its origin, its headquarters, its environmental affinity, its warm-weather fit for EV technology, and the place where Tesla faced the least threat from the car dealers. But after Elon Musk moved Tesla's headquarters to Texas in 2021 and then declared a final death grudge with Californians and progressives (which is basically the same thing) in 2024 when he announced the move of SpaceX and X's headquarters to Texas over California's transgender policies,[11] Tesla's California romance was over. Tesla's California sales plunged 24.1 percent in the second quarter of 2024.[12] At the same time, Tesla's national EV market share fell below 50 percent for the first time.[13]

Market leader Tesla may be hitting speed bumps, but other EV manufacturers are catching up. While Tesla went into reverse, six of the ten largest EV manufacturers (Hyundai/Kia, Ford, Rivian, Mercedes, BMW, and Toyota) saw their sales surge.[14] Even if Tesla recovers its mojo, other manufacturers – both legacy and start-up – were always going to close the gap. We are entering the phase where EVs will no longer be associated principally with Tesla. How that will change the direct sales equation is anyone's guess.

The most likely scenario is that things will trundle along on a state-by-state basis as they have throughout the history of the American automobile industry. We saw in Chapter 7 that the Obama Administration – not known to be especially a champion of states' rights – demurred on entering the direct sales wars on the ground that it's a state matter. In the next few years, expect to see a combination of court decisions and battles in state capitols shift the ground further toward direct sales for all EV start-ups. And, if those changes don't occur, expect to see Tesla joined by other EV start-ups in going around the remaining direct sales prohibitions and locating on tribal lands. Meanwhile, expect to see consumers in states where Tesla or other EV start-ups are shut out become increasingly vocal with their elected officials about why they can't have the same rights that consumers in most states now enjoy, and, by the way, why are you making me drive for sales or service to tribal lands where this state's coffers aren't getting any revenues?

There's also the possibility of federal action. As we saw in Chapter 1, there is precedent for federal legislation regulating automobile sales in the form of the Automobile Dealers' Day in Court Act of 1956. Congress clearly has the power to regulate automobile distribution under its commerce clause authority in Article I, Section 8, of the Constitution. There are few more obvious "instrumentalities of interstate commerce"[15] than cars. Congress already regulates motor vehicle safety comprehensively through the National Traffic and Motor Vehicle Safety Act and the National Highway Traffic Safety Administration ("NHTSA"). If a federal administration decided to throw its weight behind direct sales, it could put pressure on the hold-out states through any number of regulatory and political channels. It could prompt Congress to condition highway or other funding on liberalization of state franchise dealer laws. It could further throw the weight of the federal antitrust agencies behind arguments that particular state laws are anticompetitive. It could use the resources of the Departments of Energy or Transportation or the Environmental Protection Agency in countless ways to pressure recalcitrant states to mend their ways.

Congress could also cut through the Gordian Knot of state franchise dealer laws through an even more radical approach – a federal licensing program for dealers. There are already federal chartering or licensing programs in place for all manner of businesses, from firearms dealers to banks. I have drafted legislation that Congress could adopt to end the direct sales wars once and for all. Under my proposed bill, states could continue to license and regulate car dealers as they will, but a separate federal licensing regime would be created for companies that want to opt into a federal license (in the same way that banks can opt into a federal rather than state charter). Different kinds of companies – including manufacturers or third-party dealers – could apply for a federal license. They would have to meet the same sorts of eligibility requirements – showing things like financial responsibility and compliance with applicable laws and regulations – as states typically require of dealer licensees, with the one exception that manufacturers would also be allowed to apply. Applicants could apply for a license to sell cars, service cars, or both. Licensing fees would support a group of federal bureaucrats to administer the program and regulate the dealers. (Those who worry about creating more federal bureaucrats should remember that this program would be voluntary – companies would be opting to be regulated by federal rather than state bureaucrats.) Federally licensed dealers would be subject to all of the same consumer protection and environmental regulations that apply to other dealers, like lemon laws or financing regulations. They would have to comply with state and local zoning laws, and all applicable state and federal laws regulating labor and employment. But what the states could not do is block a federally licensed dealer from setting up a store or service center just because they were owned or operated by a manufacturer. Direct sales could come to all.

I am not Pollyanna. This is probably not going to happen. See the discussion on the politics of direct sales in Chapter 7. But at least it's useful as a thought experiment. Direct sales is a national issue. The market penetration of EVs is a national issue. Indeed, it's a global issue that relates to our most pressing debates around climate change, energy policy, the shrinking US manufacturing industry, blue-collar jobs, technological innovation, the future of the US auto industry, and the standing of the United States in the world. Whether or not the solution lies at the federal level, urgent thinking on these questions needs to happen by the smartest minds across the country.

While smart minds are contemplating the future of automobile distribution, they also need to be thinking about even bigger questions.

Other technological trends than EVs are already starting to put pressure on the dealership model. Ride-sharing services like Uber and Lyft are making it possible for people to rely on someone else's car for their transportation needs. While the empirical evidence of ride sharing on individual vehicle ownership remains mixed, it only makes sense that as more and more people rely more and more on ride-sharing services, they will buy fewer cars for themselves. This is different than saying that vehicle ownership will go down. Some studies have found that vehicle ownership actually increases with Uber or Lyft's entry into an urban area, since Uber and Lyft drivers buy cars to meet the growing demand for ride sharing.[16] For now, the predominant ride-sharing model is for individual drivers to own their own cars, which means buying from a dealer. But that could change. The car manufacturers are looking for ways to adapt to ride sharing by launching their own ride-sharing platforms (as GM did with its short-lived Maven initiative),[17] partnering with existing ride-sharing companies like Uber and Lyft, or partnering with technology companies like Google. From my conversations with industry insiders, there's an expectation that the ride-sharing model will increasingly move away from individual vehicle ownership and in the direction of fleet ownership and management. And that, in turn, raises the question of what role there is for the dealers in automobile sales. Why do GM and Lyft need dealer involvement for their fleet of self-driving electric taxis?[18]

The point about self-driving taxis brings up another whole question. If you thought EVs were a revolutionary technology, wait until we get into artificial intelligence-driven connected and autonomous vehicles. For about as long as I've been involved in the direct sales issue, I've had the privilege of learning from some of the smartest minds at work on driverless cars under the auspices of the University of Michigan's Mcity, an interdisciplinary public–private partnership and autonomous driving testing facility that brings together thought leaders from industry, government, and academia. While driverless cars have been much hyped, the public's breathless and conflicted anticipation of full self-driving vehicles that can go anywhere at any time without human direction – what the Society of Automotive Engineers ("SAE") calls Level 5 autonomy – remains a distant and ephemeral vision. But long before the fleet flips to Level 5, we will move through levels of advanced driver assistance ("ADAS"), conditional driving autonomy, and vehicle autonomy limited to increasingly broadened operational design domains. And not only will cars be increasingly robotic, they will be increasingly connected to roadside infrastructure, computer networks, and other cars on the road.

All of this is already in full swing, and before long it's going to have major implications for how cars are sold, serviced, owned, and driven. An analyst at the Plant Moran consulting firm has predicted that driverless cars could mean more sales for dealers, since although fewer individuals may own vehicles, vehicles as a whole will be used more, which means that they will need to be replaced more.[19] But that assumes that the increasing number of vehicle sales will be channeled through dealers. If the car manufacturers are running their own self-driving cars on ride-sharing platforms that they own or in partnerships with other technology companies, where's the need for the middleman to sell the car? It seems far more likely that the dealers will get cut out altogether. And if there's no sales transaction, there's no plausible argument that the manufacturers are breaking franchise dealer laws. Those laws have never said that a manufacturer has to sell a car to itself through a dealer before using it.

There are many different ways the future of riding-sharing and driverless cars could go, not to mention public transportation, micro-mobility, and urban planning and design, all of which could have dramatic effects on how cars are bought, sold, owned, operated, serviced, and shared. Looking down the road, the dealers have bigger fish to fry than the vestigial laws regulating direct sales. Instead of trying to insist that car sales should continue to be regulated by 1950s laws founded on entirely different economic, technological, and political circumstances, the car dealers need to focus on how they will be able to add real value to car manufacturers, fleet operators, state and local governments, and consumers in the changing ecosystem ahead. Almost no one involved in the direct sales debate is arguing that the coming ecosystem should be entirely unregulated (although I will have to defer to my libertarian friends). The question is what sorts of regulations (including the decision not to regulate) can best promote technological advancement, environmental protection, equity, competition, consumer choice, and the myriad of other important values that we care about as a society. The dealers have been fighting a rearguard action. It's time for them and the rest of those involved to focus on the future.

The dealers need to be part of the conversation. They need to come to the table in good faith to discuss the future rather than the past. To date, my impression is that many of the dealers have hunkered down behind their lobbyists' talking points rather than thinking critically through the issues. A good case in point occurred in the early years of the direct sales wars when I received a voicemail from someone identifying himself as affiliated with the Michigan auto dealers' association. He said that he had read some of my public statements on direct sales and suggested that we meet so that I could hear the car dealers' perspective. I called back and left my own voicemail thanking him for the invitation, saying that I would be very happy to sit down and talk, but that it would need to be an open exchange of views and not just a chance for the dealers to deliver their talking points. I never heard back.

As we close this book, I'd like to offer an olive branch. Throughout this book and in much of my work in the last decade, I've been sharply critical of the car dealers. While the dealers' lobbyists may prefer sound bites to deep conversation, and I obviously disagree with many of their arguments and some of their business, legal, and political tactics, I don't think that the dealers are bad people. There is far too much demonization of those "on the other side" in America today. We should be able to disagree, even sharply, without calling other people names or assuming the worst of them. While there are probably some rotten apples among the car dealers, there are some rotten apples among law professors too. There are also lots of good apples among the car dealers (and law professors). I think of Sigmund and Rose Strochlitz and Whaling City Ford introduced in Chapter 1. Most car dealers are just people trying to run a business, make a living, and support their families. Many are honest and hardworking men and women who are pillars of their communities, help people in need, and bring lots of value to customers who want cars. They march in the Memorial Day parade, support the Boy Scouts, pay their taxes, and treat their employees decently. I bet they love their children too.

I hope that the independent franchised dealer doesn't disappear from the American landscape. I hope to continue to see Ford, Chevy, and Toyota dealerships in the suburban strip malls. Maybe Tesla will eventually follow Apple's dual-distribution model, as we saw him hint at in Chapter 2, and we'll see some Tesla franchised dealerships crop up. But I also hope that, before long, the choice of how I buy a car will be mine, not the government's. I'd like to think that I'll never again have to haggle over price with a salesperson with well-coiffed hair and pearly white teeth. I also hope that those who love to haggle, and are better at it than I am, will be able to find outlets in which to dicker to their hearts' content. I hope I'll have the choice to customize a car online and have it delivered where I want from any manufacturer, legacy or new. In short, I hope to have the freedom to buy, and that others have that freedom too.

To return to the beginning of this chapter, the story of how Tesla went straight to the consumer and smashed the car dealers' monopoly is uniquely American. I've invested a lot in it over the last decade and sometimes have to remind myself that direct sales is far from our most pressing issue as a country. But it is an important, if frequently misunderstood, issue with a rich history, fascinating alliances, and larger-than-life characters. I hope that this book has made some contribution to explaining where the issue came from, where we are today, and what may lie in the road ahead.

Notes

1. "Say Hello to Waymo," Waymo, www.youtube.com/watch?v=uHbMt6WDhQ8.
2. Breana Noble, "Stellantis Says Direct Sales Model Could Be a 'win-win-win.' Dealers Aren't Sure," The Detroit News, April 5, 2022, www.detroitnews.com/story/business/autos/chrysler/2022/04/05/stellantis-tesla-direct-sales-model-dealers/7067748001/.
3. "Electric Vehicles and Consumer Choice: A Critical Policy Opportunity for Expanding EV Adoption," Electrification Coalition, https://electrificationcoalition.org/work/state-ev-policy/evs-and-consumer-choice/ (last visited February 16, 2025)
4. Ibid.
5. *United States* v. *Aluminum Company of America*, 148 F 2d 416, 427 (2d Cir. 1945).
6. Catherine York, "GM North America President: 'Dealers Are a Competitive Advantage,'" NADA, March 27, 2024, www.nada.org/nada/nada-headlines/gm-north-america-president-dealers-are-competitive-advantage.

7. James C. McGrath & Katherine R. Moskop, "Dealer Challenges to Ford EV Sales Requirements Continue to Mount, But Are Slow to Progress," Seyfarth, August 22, 2023, www.seyfarth.com/news-insights/dealer-challenges-to-ford-ev-sales-requirements-continue-to-mount-but-are-slow-to-progress.html.
8. Ibid.
9. "A Record 1.2 Million EVs Were Sold in the U.S. in 2023, According to Estimates from Kelley Blue Book," Cox Automotive, January 9, 2024, www.coxautoinc.com/market-insights/q4-2023-ev-sales/.
10. "Why Are EV Sales Slowing?," Goldman Sachs, May 21, 2024, www.goldmansachs.com/intelligence/pages/why-are-ev-sales-slowing.html.
11. Ramishah Maruf, "Elon Musk Says He's Moving SpaceX and X Out of California," CNN, July 16, 2024, www.cnn.com/2024/07/16/business/elon-musk-spacex-x-texas/index.html.
12. Russ Mitchell, "Statewide EV Sales Growth Sees a Drop. Tesla, Once a California Darling, Hit Hard," Los Angeles Times, July 18, 2024, www.latimes.com/environment/story/2024-07-18/california-ev-sales-decline-again.
13. Al Root, "Tesla's Market Share Is Below 50%. Here's the Upside.," Barron's, July 14, 2024, www.barrons.com/articles/tesla-market-share-falls-upside-competition-97442f72.
14. Tom Randall, "The Slowdown in US Electric Vehicle Sales Looks More like a Blip," Bloomberg, May 28, 2024, www.bloomberg.com/news/articles/2024-05-28/the-slowdown-in-us-electric-vehicle-sales-looks-more-like-a-blip.
15. *United States* v. *Lopez*, 514 U.S. 549, 558 (1995) ("Congress is empowered to regulate and protect the instrumentalities of interstate commerce, or persons or things in interstate commerce, even though the threat may come only from intrastate activities.").
16. Jacob W. Ward, et al., "The Impact of Uber and Lyft on Vehicle Ownership, Fuel Economy and Transit across U.S. Cities" (2021) 24 iScience, www.ncbi.nlm.nih.gov/pmc/articles/PMC7835256/.
17. Laura Sky Brown, "GM's Car-Sharing Service, Maven, Shuts Down after Four Years," Car & Driver, April 22, 2020, www.caranddriver.com/news/a32235218/gm-maven-car-sharing-closes/.
18. Kara Swisher & Mark Bergen, "GM Invests $500 million in Lyft and Strikes Strategic Autonomous Car Alliance," Vox, January 4, 2016, www.vox.com/2016/1/4/11588444/gm-invests-500-million-in-lyft-and-strikes-strategic-autonomous-car.
19. Steve Finlay, "Fewer Vehicles, More Sales in Autonomous Age," Wards Auto, February 1, 2022, www.wardsauto.com/financials/fewer-vehicles-more-sales-in-autonomous-age.

INDEX

Aaron Miller, 94
Acadia Center, 108
Afeela, 82
Aiosa, Jeff, 152
Alabama, 115, 150
Alaska, 153
Alliance for Automotive Innovation, 146
Alliance for Clean Energy New York, 108
Amazon, 129
American Antitrust Institute, 112
American Council for an Energy-Efficient Economy, 108
Americans for Prosperity, 5, 105, 110–111
Apple, 33, 55
Appleton, Jim, 38–40
Aptera Motors, 5, 34, 135
Arizona, 127, 149
Arizona Department of Transportation, 149
Arkansas, 41, 115, 150–151, 161
Arrival, 34–35, 132–133
Aston Martin, 25
Australia, 158
Autoline Daily, 33
Automobile Dealers' Day in Court Act of 1956, 17, 164
Automotive News, 82, 145
Automotive Trade Association, 82
AutoNation, 44, 49, 55
   CEO Mike Jackson's argument for allowing direct sales, 49
Ayres, Ian, 61

Barra, Mary, 72, 80
battery range, 129
Beijing Auto Show, 26
Berger-Girvalo, Aimee, 120
Better Business Bureau, 32

Beyer, Don, 47
Bezos, Jeff, 120
Biden, Joe, 120
Biden Administration, 67, 79, 116–117, 121, 151
Bieber, Justin, 25
Big Three, 2, 14–15, 17, 19–20, 87–88, 96, 158
BlackRock, 133
Bloomberg, 38
Bloomberg study, 143
BMW, 25, 44, 163
Bollinger Motors, 34, 135
Brandeis, Louis, 15
British Columbia, 132
Buchanan, Vern, 47
Bureau of Labor Statistics, 65
Burns, Terry, 90

California, 20, 41, 94, 120, 129, 132–133, 135, 141, 145–146, 159, 163
California Air Resources Board, 79
California New Car Dealers Association, 145
CALSTART, 108
Canada, 158
Carmody, Ellen, 97
Carter, Bob, 83
CBS News, 93
Chen, Jim, 130, 136
Chevrolet, 31
China, 80–81, 158
Christie, Chris, 38, 40, 115
Chrysler, 14, 44, 75
   in 1939 FTC report, 16
   Justice Department accusations against, 17
   merger with Dodge, 14

Index

Chrysler Dodge Jeep RAM SRT, 47
CNN, 93
Coda Automotive, 25–26
Collection Auto Group, 47
Collegio, Jonathan, 57
Colorado, 132, 146
  direct sales bill, 78–79
Commerce Clause, 95, 164
Compaq Computers, 55
competition
  competitive markets, 58
  interbrand vs. intrabrand, 42, 59
Connecticut, 19, 115, 144, 150–152
Connecticut League of Conservation Voters, 108
Consumer Action, 5, 53, 109
Consumer Federation of America, 5, 32, 53, 60, 109
consumer protection, 20
Consumer Reports, 2, 24, 30, 73, 132
consumer rights, 53
Consumers for Auto Reliability and Safety, 52, 109
Coppola, Francis Ford, 14
Cournot, Augustin, 59
COVID, 98–99
Customergauge, 143
Cyrill, Charles, 57

David Sappington, 62
dealer protection laws, 18
dealers
  accusations against in 1939 FTC report, 16
  advertising, 30
  bargaining power, 44
  conflict of interest, 30
  employment data, 159
  employment statistics, 65
  inventory model, 28
  lack of consumer trust, 32
  as mom-and-pops, 3, 43–44, 74
  number of, 13–14
  philanthropy, 67
  profit model, 29–30
  store locations, 27
Delaware, 141, 148
Dell Computers, 55
Democratic Party, 87, 90, 99–100, 107
Department of Energy, 117
Department of Transportation, 117, 164

Departments of Energy, 164
Departments of Justice, 117
DeSantis, Ron, 146
Detroit, 25, 72
Detroit Auto Show, 94
DiCaprio, Leonardo, 25
double marginalization, 59
driverless cars, 157, 166

electric vehicles, sales data, 163
Electrification Coalition, 118, 132, 137, 159
Elio Motors, 127–128
energy independence, 4
Environment America, 5, 108
environmental groups, 78
environmental issues, 4
Environmental Protection Agency, 79, 108, 117, 164
equal protection clause, 96, 137
Europe, 158
EV mandates, 79–80
EVHybridNoire, 114
Experian, 143
Exxon, 95

Faraday, Michael, 135
Faraday Future, 34, 135
Farley, Jim, 81
Federal Reserve Bank of Chicago, 61
Federal Trade Commission, 27, 53–55, 59, 117, 145, 148
  1939 report, 15–18
  direct sales hearings, 127
  enforcement of Magnuson-Moss Act, 62
Financial Crisis of 2008–2009, 73
first mover advantage and disadvantage, 125
Fisker, Henrik, 25, 34
Fisker Automotive, 26, 34
Fisker Inc., 35, 135
  bankruptcy, 35
  Fisker Ocean, 35
Fisker Motors, 25, 63
Florida, 80, 146, 161
Florida Automobile Dealers Association, 61
Forbes, 29
Ford, 4, 14, 44, 146, 161, 163
  1916 proposal to create retail stores, 18
  in 1939 FTC report, 16
  assembly-line production, 11
  constitutional challenge in Texas, 95
  decision to back dealers, 75

Index

direct sales in China, 81
direct sales in Texas in 1990s, 20–21
flexible sales strategy, 81
investment in Rivian, 80, 129
Justice Department accusations against, 17
merger with Lincoln, 14
Model E, 81, 161
Model T, 13
opposition to Michigan legislation codifying Tesla settlement, 100
support for anti-Tesla legislation in Michigan, 91
Ford, Henry, 13
France, 80

Gateway Computers, 55, 87
GeekWire, 136
General Motors, 4, 11, 14, 44, 64, 160, 162
in 1939 FTC report, 16
Cadillac dealer buyouts, 80
Cadillac Lyriq, 80
Chevy Bolt, 77
Colorado strategy, 78
decision to back dealers, 76
direct sales dilemma, 72
direct sales in Brazil, 56
direct-to-consumer model, 80
discontinuation of Oldsmobile brand, 25
EV1, 77
Maven, 166
merger with Opel, 14
opposition to Michigan legislation codifying Tesla settlement, 100
strategy against Tesla in Ohio, 76
support for anti-Tesla legislation in Michigan, 91
Georgia, 41, 132, 147, 162
gigafactory, 147
Gillis, Jack, 60
GM, Justice Department accusations against, 17
Goldman Sachs, 55, 163
Google, 126, 157
Gore, Al, 25
Great Atlantic & Pacific Tea Company, 15
Great Depression, 13–15
Group 1 Automotive, 44

haggling over prices, 60–61
Haley, Nikki, 116

Hand, Learned, 159
Harris Poll, 32
Hawaii, 153
Hawley, Josh, 148
Henry, Jim, 29
Hollywood, 25
Honda, 31–32, 44, 81
Hune, John, 89, 97
Hyundai, 62
Hyundai/Kia, 44, 163

Idaho, 153
Illinois, 129, 132, 148, 161
Illinois Automobile Dealers Association, 148
Indiana, 75, 78–79, 147
Information Technology and Innovation Foundation, 113
Luddite award, 93
Institute for Justice, 5, 110
International Brotherhood of Electrical Workers, 114
International Center for Law and Economics, 110
International Harvester, 82
Iowa, 150

Jaguar, 44
Jonas, Joe, 25
Justice Department, 17, 54, 59, 134
white paper on direct sales, 55

Kansas, 150
Kasich, John, 76–77
Kelly, Mike, 47
Ken Garff Automotive Group, 44–45
Kentucky, 19, 41, 149–150
Keogh, Scott, 135
Kessler, Glenn, 56
Koch Brothers, 105–106. *See also* Americans for Prosperity
Krattenmaker, Tom, 77
Kutcher, Ashton, 25

labor unions, 14
Lamar Bus Company, 78
Law and Political Economy movement, 67
Lordstown Motors, 34–35, 135
Lotus, 24
Louisiana, 19, 115, 127, 134, 142, 150
Louisiana Automobile Dealers Association, 63

Louisiana Motor Vehicle Commission, 63
Lucid, 5, 7, 34, 134–135, 148, 151, 162
   ratings in U.S. News & World Report, 62
Lucid Motors, 133–134
Lyft, 166

Macaulay, Stewart, 17
Mackinac Center, 87, 110
MAGA, 116, 163
Magnuson-Moss Act, 62
Mahan, Steve, 157
Maine, 153
Marcetic, Branko, 105
Maron, Todd, 27, 91, 141–142, 144
Maryland, 95, 137, 147
Massachusetts, 41, 148
   Supreme Court decision, 89, 149
   Supreme Court direct sales decision, 41–43
Mazda, 44
McCormick, Kathaleen, 141
McElroy, John, 33
Mercatus Center, 110
Mercedes-Benz, 44, 129, 163
Michigan, 19, 41, 44, 54, 75, 78, 79, 112, 128–129, 135–136, 144, 148, 168
   constitutional prohibition on special acts, 100
   direct sales battles, 87–102
   Flint water crisis, 93
   House Government Operations Committee, 99
   legislative history of direct sales ban, 88
   Office of Investigative Services Business Compliance and Regulation Division, 94
   tax revenues from car sales, 66
Michigan Auto Dealers Association, 90
Michigan Conservation Voters, 108
Mickelson, Phil, 25
Minnesota, 148
Minnesota Department of Public Safety, 148
Mississippi, 48, 115, 134, 137, 147
Mississippi Automobile Dealers Association, 48
Missouri, 41, 43, 148
Missouri Department of Revenue, 148
Mitsubishi, 44, 129
Mobil Corporation, 138
Mohegan tribe, 152
mom-and-pops, 111

monopoly, 113
   vertical monopoly, 57
Montana, 150
Montgomery Ward, 11, 138
Moreno, Bernie, 47
Motor Trend, 133
Musk, Elon, 21, 55
   changes in policies, 144
   compensation package, 141
   direct sales decision, 24–35
   hostility toward, 99
   marriages and divorces, 141
   on Tesla's no-discounting policy, 60
   Personality, 3
   polarizing figure, 107
   political controversy, 120
   relationship with Donald Trump, 121
   titles with Tesla, 26
   Wealth, 4

Nader, Ralph, 52
Nambé Pueblo, 152
National Association of Automobile Dealers, 15
National Association of Automotive Data, data on car dealers, 45
National Association of Automotive Dealers, 83, 147, 160
   arguments against direct sales, 57
   fact-checking DOJ white paper on direct sales, 56
   national convention, 116
   political contributions, 46
   threatened lawsuit against Honda and Volkswagen, 82
National Automobile Dealers Association, 159
   annual convention, 31
National Fair Housing Alliance, 61
National Highway Traffic Safety Administration, 64, 164
National Industrial Recovery Act, 15
National Public Radio, 33
National Traffic and Motor Vehicle Safety Act, 164
Nebraska, 150
Nessel, Dana, 97
Nevada, 110, 147, 162
New Bridge Strategy, 118
New Deal, 17, 95
New Hampshire, 41, 146
New Jersey, 7, 38–41, 115, 147

Index

Division of Consumer Affairs, 40
Motor Vehicle Commission, 38
New Jersey Coalition of Automotive Retailers, 38
New Mexico, 150, 152
New York, 41, 43, 115, 132, 136, 147, 152, 161–162
New York League of Conservation Voters, 108
Nikola Motors, 34, 135
Nissan, 31, 44
North Carolina, 118, 137, 147, 161
North Dakota, 150
Nu Ride. *See* Lordstown Motors

O'Connell, Diarmuid, 33
Obama, Barack, 117
Obama Administration, 117, 164
Ohio, 41, 47, 75, 79, 135, 137
service centers close to Michigan, 94
Ohio Bureau of Motor Vehicles, 76
Ohio laws, 147
Oklahoma, 17, 150
Oneida nation, 152
Open Secrets, 46
Oregon, 153
over-the-air updates, 131

PayPal, 24
Pelican Institute for Public Policy, 110
Pennsylvania, 137, 147, 162
Penske Automotive Group, 29, 44
Pep Boys, 127
Perry, Rick, 115
Pininfarina, 26
Plant Moran, 167
Plug In America, 108
Pohanka, Geoffrey, 82
Powell, Colin, 25
public choice theory, 47
Public Interest Research Group, 108
public opinion polls, 46, 118–119

racial and gender discrimination, 60–61
raising rivals' costs, 77
Rambo, Dave, 61
Reeves, Tate, 147
Republican Party, 76, 87, 89–90, 94, 99–101, 107, 116, 128, 147
dealer donations to, 46
Reuters, 93
Rhode Island, 149

Riley, Talulah, 141
Rivian, 5, 7, 34, 136, 148, 162–163
Colorado strategy, 78
company origins, 125
customer satisfaction, 132
electric delivery vehicle, 129
Ford investment, 81, 129
presence in Michigan, 88
R1S, 128
ratings in U.S. News & World Report, 62
reasons for direct sales strategy, 130–131
stock price, 129, 131
Volkswagen investment, 129
Road and Track, 93
Robinson-Patman Act, 15
Roosevelt, Franklin, 95
R-Street, 110
Rubio, Marco, 115

safety recalls, 64
Salop, Steve, 77
Sammon, Alexander, 31, 116
Sanders, Bernie, 120
Santa Ana Pueblo, 152
Santa Clara Valley Blind Center, 157
Sardinas, Paula, 137
Saudi Arabia, 133
Save the Sound, 108
Scaringe, RJ, 125–126
Schauer, Mark, 87
Scott Morton, Fiona, 134
Scout Motors, 5, 34, 82
Sears, Roebuck and Company, 11
Securing America's Future Energy, 113
Securities and Exchange Commission, 120
service centers, 63
Shahan, Rosemary, 52–53, 161
Sheppard, Jason, 97
Sierra Club, 5, 31, 105, 108–109
Silicon Valley, 73
Silver, Nate, 116
Slate, 31, 116
Sloan, Alfred P., 12–13, 25, 32
Small Business Administration, 45
Snyder, Rick, 87–94
Society of Automotive Engineers, 166
Sonic Automotive, 44
Sony, 82
South Carolina, 115, 150
South Dakota, 150, 161
SpaceX, 24, 163
State Street, 133

Stellantis Group, 146. *See also* Chrysler
Stevens, John Paul, 95
Strochlitz, Rose and Sigmund, 9–11, 14, 168
Subaru, 33, 44
Suburban Collection, 44
Supreme Court, on interbrand vs. intrabrand competition, 59
Sweden, 80
Switzerland, 80

tax revenues, 66–67
Tennessee, 132, 153
Tennessee Funeral Directors and Embalmers Act, 96
Tesla
  Ann Arbor, Michigan store, 101
  Colorado opening, 78
  constitutional challenge in Michigan, 95–98
  customer loyalty, 142–143
  Cyber Truck, 119
  Department of Energy loans, 110
  EV tax credits, 110
  gigafactory, 110
  having a monopoly, 39
  Liberating American consumer, 2
  managerial turnover, 144
  market capitalization, 73
  market share losses due to Musk's politics, 163
  Michigan settlement, 97
  Model 3, 40
  Model S, 2, 14, 24
  number of sales centers, 142
  number of service centers, 142
  ratings in U.S. News & World Report, 62
  Roadster, 24
  sales centers, 5
  service centers, 6
Tesla, Nikola, 135
Texas, 19, 95, 110, 115, 129, 132, 134, 150–151, 157, 163
  Motor Vehicle Board, 21
Texas Auto Dealer Association, 57
Texas Automobile Dealers Association, 63, 134
Texas Department of Motor Vehicles, 134

Timex, 113
Toyota, 31, 44, 74, 83, 163
tribal lands, 151–153
Trump, Donald, 76, 116
Trump Administration, 79, 109

Uber, 166
Ukraine, 120
United Auto Workers, 88, 100
United Auto Workers Union, 114
University of Michigan, 39, 87, 166
U.S. News & World Report, 62
Utah, 41, 146

Vanguard Group, 133
Vermont, 41
vertical integration, 59
VinFast, 34
Virginia, 19, 41, 149–150
Volkswagen, 74, 81, 129, 135
  Cupra EV, 82
Volkswagen-Audi, 44
Volvo, 44, 81

Wagoner, Rick, 25
Wall Street Journal, 75, 93, 129
warranties, 61–62
Warren, Elizabeth, 120
Washington, 41, 132, 136–137, 147, 162
Washington Build Back Black Alliance, 137
Washington Post, 56
Waymo. *See* Google
West, Marissa, 160
West Virginia, 41, 115, 131, 150–151
Wetzel, Jason, 75
Whaling City Ford. *See* Strochlitz, Rose and Sigmund
Whitmer, Gretchen, 97–98
Williams, Roger, 47
Wilson, Justine, 141
Wisconsin, 17, 19–20, 41, 149–150
Wolters, Bill, 57
Wyoming, 41, 146

X, 163

Yugo, 26

For EU product safety concerns, contact us at Calle de José Abascal, 56–1°, 28003 Madrid, Spain or eugpsr@cambridge.org.

www.ingramcontent.com/pod-product-compliance
Lightning Source LLC
LaVergne TN
LVHW011829060526
838200LV00053B/3952